The Twelve Steps to A Meaningful Life

In the long run, a person who goes
The second mile will be further ahead

D1508899

Edward L. Roth, CFP®

Dedication

Introduction to the book, *"The Twelve Steps to a Meaningful Life."*

The Purpose and goal of writing this book is to be a source of encouragement to my children, grandchildren, and great grandchildren and dedicate it to my wife and partner these past 65 years. Without her loving support, it would have been impossible to have a rewarding life that I have lived. This book is dedicated to Mildred L Bontrager Roth, who is the love of my life.

Registered Principal

Raymond James Financial Services, Inc.

Member FINRA/SIPC phone: 419-446-2701 fax: 419-445-3607 103 Main Street

P.O. Box 53129

Pettisville, OH 43553-0129

Edward.Roth@Raymondjames.com

About the Author

My parents, Reuben and Norma Roth, started their married life on January 26, 1928, in Milford, Nebraska. They moved that year to Alberta, Canada, and homesteaded on the prairie in Western Alberta. I remember my father telling me that the first building they built was a granary because they wanted to make sure they had storage for the grain harvest in the fall. So they lived in the granary until the house was built. That is where I learned about hard work and core values.

In 1941, my family moved to Northwest Ohio to establish a life in the USA. My first business experience was a Newspaper route at age 10. From a very young age, I was taught that a person must be independent and resourceful enough to be in business for yourself. I quickly learned that not everyone pays on time.

This book is sharing what some of my failures were, and that failure is a stepping stone in life. It is through failure that we learn to be successful. For every adversity, there is a seed of an equivalent or greater benefit. It is my goal to help the reader understand the truth of life that will help them have a more meaningful life and to learn from some of the hard lessons of life. There will always be a calm before the storm, or the storm that comes after the calm in our lives. However, if we have no rain, we would soon live in a desert.

*"The greater danger for most of us lies not in setting our aim too high and falling short; but in setting our aim too low, and achieving our mark." - **Michelangelo***

Acknowledgment

A special thank you to Irene Pearson and her team for their professional help in creating this book. They are the greatest writing couches a person can have. If you have an idea for a book, it is my recommendation you consult with Irene Pearson and her team.

About the Author

Edward L. Roth, CFP®

Registered Principal

Mr. Roth, Branch Manager, is a registered principal, a registered options principal, a licensed insurance agent, and a registered investment advisor representative. He is a

CERTIFIED FINANCIAL PLANNER™ professional; member of the Institute of CERTIFIED FINANCIAL PLANNERS™, and a past board member of the local chapter of the International Association of Financial Planners.

Ed is the president of Northwest Investment Co., general partner of O'Artic Investment Co. and the president of Roth, Britsch, Dickman, Inc. DBA: Investment Planning Associates, an independent practice*. He is also a past Vice-President of Ethics for the board of the Northwest Ohio FPA (Financial Planning Association).

He worked in consumer finance for 15 years prior to his 47 years of experience in the financial field.

Ed and his wife, Millie, reside in rural Archbold, Ohio, and are the proud parents of seven children and thirteen grandchildren and four Great-grandchildren.

His office is located at 103 Main Street, Pettisville, OH 43553.

Ed is a graduate of the New York Institute of

Finance and the Investment Training

Preface

In a world full of competitors, become a successful person. The meaning of success may vary from person to person and depends on a lot of factors. Success is not just about becoming a millionaire or doing whatever it takes to get rich. Sometimes success is all about having a roof over your head and not having a thing to worry about at all. Or becoming a helping hand that can guide others when they are lost.

This world is not as complicated as people make it out to be. Some of the complications we see prevailing in this world are due to our actions and nothing more. Our actions come with consequences, and some of these consequences can prove to be fatal for us. I am writing this book to help people simplify their complicated lives, and help them understand that success is not the only thing we need to strive for in this world. We need to strive for a better version of ourselves with every step we take in this world.

Contents

Dedication i
About the Author ii
Acknowledgment iv
About the Author vi
Preface viii

Chapter 1 1
Live A Simple Life ....
Chapter 2 17
Spend Less and Save More ....
Chapter 3 - Part I 36
Think Constructively ....
Chapter 3 - Part II 48
How to Build Emotional Quotient ....
Chapter 4 56
Creating A Yielding Disposition ....
Chapter 5 70
Be Grateful ....
Chapter 6 86
Rule Your Moods ....
Chapter 7 103
Giving Generously ....
Chapter 8 117
Motives Matter ....
Chapter 9 129
Be Interested In Others ....
Chapter 10 140
Live One Day at a Time ....
Chapter 11 151
Hobbies ....
Chapter 12 159
Always Keep Close to God ....

Page Left Blank Intentionally

Chapter 1
Live A Simple Life

The world we live in today is far different than the world in the past centuries. Today, people tend to be busier than ever and barely have time even for their families. Their excuses lie in earning more money because we believe earning more money can bring us more comfort. However, there is nothing comfortable about overworking yourself and coming home burnt out. There is nothing comfortable about coming home just to sleep. There is nothing comfortable about sacrificing your social life and family life for your professional life.

We go to work because we want to live a comfortable life, yet we allow this life to snatch our comforts for the sake of earning money. All of us are so busy trying to make a living that we have forgotten how to actually live a comfortable life. We just go into survival mode and somehow try to survive. The schedule we follow is infamously frantic. It constantly leaves us feeling pressed for time. This feeling has nothing to do with time but how we decide to spend it.

We lead a complicated life because leading a simple life is not an option most of us believe that we can afford. Most of us blame the economy for this succulent behavior of being busy with our lives, but the truth is entirely different. There is a bigger reason behind why we have busied ourselves to the point where hearing the phrase, *"I'm busy,"* does not look strange anymore. How many of us have tried to use this excuse to get out of a social gathering we do not want to attend or a party we do not want to attend due to the work we have to do? We have complicated our life and way of living because we want to feel important.

Psychologically, the reason why most people busy themselves closely relates to their psyche. None of us pays much attention to how busy we are in life. It is a topic that barely shows up in books, movies, and TV series. The truth is that we are attracted to the concept of leading a busy life. We slowly form an addiction to being busy due to the sense of achievement we feel whenever we complete a certain task at hand. Our concept of importance now lies in how busy we are with our life. *"I'm busy, so I'm more important since I have more work to do than others."*

Believe it or not, our society encourages people to be busy without realizing how damaging it can be on our psyche. We feel a sense of accomplishment when we tell people that we are too busy to attend an event or meet someone. Another reason why people tend to busy themselves is that having free time means more thinking. This thought pattern can lead them to face the truth. Some of us, if not most, want to run away from our life, so we use busyness as a scapegoat for avoiding facing the reality of our life. Free time leads to boredom, and boredom leads to self-evaluating thoughts. Most of us prefer being ignorant over going through the self-realization and self-awareness process.

Leading a busy life has become a tool of measurement. The busier you are, the more important you feel in your life. Those who have free time in their life are rendered as less important. It is an alternative way to invoke self-importance and stroke your own ego. We believe that leading a busier life equates to leading a fulfilling life. However, leading a busier life is equal to living a deprived life. We no longer spend an adequate amount of time with our families and friends. We prefer solitariness to solidarity so that we can simply catch up with ourselves. Even then, we try to search for different ways to escape.

Escaping can only lead us so far. There comes the point where everything catches up on us, and we crash under pressure. Putting off our problems in life leads to more anxiety and uneasiness in a person. We develop certain habits to keep ourselves busy. Selfishness is one of the major reasons why we try to keep ourselves busy in life.

We do not want to spare our time with others and keep everything to ourselves. Those who tend to lead a busier life like to keep their free time all to themselves. They do not like to interact with others because they need time to catch up with themselves. It is a good thing to spend some time with yourself but better to give some time to others as well.

Making Life Complicated

Most people fail to recognize that being busy is more of a decision than an option. The bad news is time flies. The good news is... you're the pilot.

Most of us confuse the word busy with productivity. However, these two terms have completely different meanings. Just because we say that life is supposed to be simple does not mean that it is going to be easy. Leading a busy life gives rise to complications that we face from time to time. These complications can be as small as not being able to meet someone you really love, or as big as abandoning people you know for other things. Lack of prioritizing things can also lead to several complications in life. It gives rise to complications in health as we overwork ourselves from time to time. We pay more bills when we are trying to earn more money. The irony of the situation catches up to us as we start losing more than gaining less.

Busyness is often associated with selfishness due to several reasons. The concept of being selfish is often looked down upon despite it being an abstract term. The main reason why most people are befuddled by the concept of selfishness is the dualistic nature of the human mind. We tend to view things in either good light or a bad one. We tend to view things from two sides. Good and bad, up and down, far and near, big and small, virtue and vice, friend and foe, and so on. Selfishness is a vast concept and cannot be fitted into two extremes. There are psychological reasons behind the selfish behavior exhibited by certain people in the world. In one way or another, we are all selfish at a certain point in our life.

We want to do things that are ultimately for our own good and well-being. This type of selfishness is categorized as a good and desirable trait. However, it is quite easy to tip the balance between good selfish behavior and toxic selfish behavior. There are times when our selfish behavior causes harm to others. The problem arises when we decide to focus solely on ourselves and do things for ourselves while disregarding others' needs. Fulfilling our needs at the expense of others is one of the most toxic traits possessed by anyone. Making life difficult for others to meet your own needs is the type of selfishness we must avoid in our life.

How to Avoid Being Selfish

As stated above, we all act selfishly at some point in our life. It is crucial to make sure that we do not fall into the toxic category. It is important to go through a self-evaluation process to make sure that our selfish behavior does not evolve into a toxic personality trait. The only way we can go through the self-evaluation process is by making sure that we have enough time on our hands. The more time we spend with ourselves, the more time we get to explore ourselves. Most of the time, we also explore certain parts of our personality that we did not know exist before we meet certain people in our lives.

Entitlement

Selfish people believe that they are entitled to everything and deserve nothing but the best in the world. They are characterized by their inconsistency when they pursue their goals. They continuously change their goals and demand every time that they are valued more and recognized as if they have spent the majority of their time pursuing a goal. The sense of entitlement is aroused due to their sense of self-importance.

This kind of behavior leads them to cross certain boundaries that should never be crossed. They do their best to get rid of those who they believe can become a hindrance as they try to achieve their goal. They disregard others completely just to reach the final step of success in their life.

Self-Centered Attitude

They believe that the world revolves around them and that everyone is there to get them. They do not accept constructive criticism because they believe that the critic is trying to devalue their work and potential. They go to great lengths to defend themselves when criticized and do whatever it takes to prove the other person wrong. They do not realize that criticism can help them recognize their flaws so that they can correct them in the future. Constructive criticism can lead to improvements and developments.

Nemesis

Those who refuse to listen to others believe that they are mature and intelligent enough. Selfish people view others as their nemesis and believe that they do not deserve their respect or attention. Learning and listening from opinions is not a trait that is possessed by selfish people, although it is proven to be good and provides us with opportunities to broaden our horizons. We should never ignore or stop listening to others simply because we view them as our enemies.

Criticizing Others

Selfish people are afraid of confronting others. They are also afraid of being confronted. They hate when others criticize them, but they love when it is their turn to criticize others. They use the cheap trick of going behind someone's back and criticizing them for the work they do on a daily basis.

Lack of Humility

One of the notorious deficiencies selfish people possess is the lack of humility. It is a precious human virtue that is needed for personal growth. It allows us to socialize appropriately within our environment. Egocentric people only cover up personal potential and look for ways to stand out. They only stand out if they amplify their achievements.

Selfish people tend to generously award themselves with more responsibility and take credit for a certain project when it becomes successful. They immediately look for many ways to disown when a project does not turn out to go well. They play the blame game   to   place   the responsibility of the failure on someone else entirely.

Playing It Safe

Believe it or not, selfish people are scared of taking risks due to the fear linked with failure. They do not consider failure as an option and decide never to expose themselves to it. They do not think twice before criticizing those who take risks in their life. They never expose themselves to risks and play it safe in life. If you have any of these traits, it means you are not taking proper responsibility for your life. You do not hold yourself accountable for everything that is going around. The behavior mentioned above leads to selfish behavior. This type of behavior can easily hurt those around us as we try to inflict the problems on others.

How to Lead a Simple Life

Leading a simple life can help a person understand the core values on which a fundamental society functions. There are many ways through which we can lead a simple life. First, we need to sort out our priorities and give more importance to others than ourselves. Then, we need to learn how to give ourselves more time. It is imperative to organize yourself and your life to lead a simple life.

Pray

Most of us do not mediate due to the busy life we lead. Praying is one of the most fulfilling factors. We should give ourselves enough time to connect with God. We are always so busy planning for this world that we do not bother planning for the world that comes after this one. The concept of the afterlife seems bogus to some people, but praying can also lead to mental peace. It gives us enough time to breathe and focus on ourselves.

Organize Time

It is imperative to organize time. Our entire life is ruled by the time we spend on this planet. Everything is scheduled according to time. It is a good thing that you want to spend more time at work, but it is crucial to allot more time for your family. Today, we focus more on providing with our family than bonding with them. Familial values are diminishing due to the fact that we do not have enough time to bond with each other. There is no time at all, and that is why it is crucial to organize our time according to our priorities.

Learn to Say No

We are taught from a young age to always say yes because saying no is seen as rude. There are some circumstances that lead us to hesitate. We give more than we take. That can prove to be harmful in the future. Saying yes to everything can potentially harm our relationship with others when we realize that we are being taken advantage of. It is crucial to say no when the need arises. Doing more than it is required only creates complications. Let's assume your friend requests you to do her part of the assignment. You agree and submit that assignment of yours in her name. Something goes wrong, and now she blames you for ruining her chances of getting a good reward. This leads to ruining your friendship as she pushes the blame onto you regardless of whether you messed it up unintentionally.

Assign Responsibilities

Assigning responsibilities to yourself and others can help you organize your time better. You do not have to do everything by yourself. It is crucial to assign responsibilities to your counterpart to make your life easier and simpler.

Declutter and Simplify

Our life is cluttered around. We need to declutter it by making a list of what is important in order to simplify it. Pull your life apart by thinking about it and come up with innovative ways to make yourself more productive and less busy.

Pace Yourself

Give yourself enough time to organize your thoughts, feelings, emotions, and life so that you can pace yourself. Give yourself the love and time you need to understand what is more important to you.

Eat Right

Due to the busy pace of our lives, we resort to canned food and microwavable goods. This can ruin your diet and affect your health. It fails to provide you with the nutritional energy you need to be more productive in life. It is important to maintain good nutrition so we can lead a healthy lifestyle. Your diet can help you maintain a healthy weight and reduce the risk of having chronic diseases linked to the heart. It promotes overall health and provides you with the energy you need to stay healthy.

Be Organized

Organize, organize, and organize. Learn how to organize everything in your life to simplify it. It helps with prioritizing what we should hold close to us and what we should let go of. Simplicity and freedom are directly proportional to each other. The more you own, the more responsibilities you have to cater to, and you will have to serve your ego more. As a result, there will be less freedom available to you.

Freedom is all about walking down the road, looking up at the sky, and doing all the things that can make you happy. A simple life gives you freedom from minor issues in life. Freedom also provides you to learn more about yourself. It gives you enough time to reevaluate your life and life choices. It provides you with time to reflect and be more grateful for what you have.

To lead a simple life, you do not have to give up on your job and profession. You simply need to organize everything according to priority. This means you need to attain mental peace. There are people who are surrounded by their families and still stress about work. They are physically present but absent mentally. Organizing your time and allotting it accordingly can help you get rid of this habit. Fewer possessions you own can lead to less clutter. Having a lower number of commitments can also do the same. Instead of cleaning your house due to the number of possessions you own, you can spend that free time, which is present at your disposal. Living a real and simple life is all about decluttering your life, prioritizing family to the profession, and being a little selfish to a healthy amount of time.

It is about time that we focus less on surviving and getting through the day and more on living our life to the fullest. Here I leave you with a few thoughts in relation to what we have just discussed in the chapter. I hope they would be of benefit to you. You may follow these thoughts while striving to live a good life.

- Money has no meaning without God.
- A little is a lot if that is all you have got.
- May you live as long as you like and have what you like as long as you live

- As you wander through life, no matter where you go, keep your eye upon the donut and not on the hole.

Chapter 2
Spend Less and Save More

"Success is not about getting what you want, but enjoying what you have."

The world runs on money since this piece of paper provides us with shelter, food, and comfort. Although some people earn enough to provide themselves with shelter and food, comfort is a factor that cannot be attained easily. The concept of comfort may be different for many people, but we know that anything that puts us at ease and makes our lives easier is qualified as a comfort.

There are two types of comfort in our lives. Worldly comfort is the one that fulfills our basic necessities in life so that we can lead our lives effectively. Then comes in personal comforts, the one we seek in this world just to seek temporary relief. Worldly comforts are different from personal comfort. If an individual earns enough to provide themselves with basic necessities and still comes home with a stable mindset, then that individual is far richer than the person who runs after money to seek a personal boost for his ego rather than opting for worldly comforts. A massage chair may provide comfort, but do we really need it in our lives? The real problem lies in the fact that not many people are able to discern between necessary comforts and excessive comforts. There are some necessities that we cannot live without. We cannot live without water, nor can we live without electricity. These align with comforts necessary in life, but then there are other comforts that are not necessarily needed, but we still seek them out for one reason or another. We are always busy to live out our best life today that we forget to plan for tomorrow.

According to psychology, individuals have a certain blind spot when it comes to thinking about their future and finances. Intellectually smart people with a perfectly planned balance sheet also tend to have desires and fall into these blind spots like any average person that lacks skills to balance out their lives. Despite their clear understanding, they tend to forget about checking in on their savings from time to time to make sure they have enough in their pockets. There comes a breaking point where they give in to their desires and spend the money they placed in their savings accounts to buy something completely unnecessary in life.

This can lead to harmful results as it creates a sense of false security in an individual.

Why do we spend excessively?

Most of us spend excessively to maintain a certain type of lifestyle. Our childhood is partly to blame for it. No one teaches us about the importance of money from a very young age. Parents do not provide the child with a valid reason when they tell them to put a certain item away. This is only because they feel ashamed of openly talking about financial strain with their children, and avoiding topics like the plague. Therefore, children form an ideal lifestyle as they transition from childhood to adulthood without realizing how many responsibilities lie behind their comfortable life.

We get exposure when we walk into the real world of finances. The responsibilities are overwhelming at first, and usually, individuals do not know how to differentiate between necessities and accessories. We have all made a mistake with handling our finances here and there, but we move on by telling ourselves that we can only learn from these mistakes. However, there are many reasons why people spend their money excessively.

Lack of Future Planning

Thinking about the future can be scary sometimes. We all abide by a general rule of dealing with the future when it arrives. The future is uncertain, and none of us can accurately predict how much we will spend in the future. However, thinking about the future is one of the key components of taking on financial responsibility. We have the tendency to focus on our present and do not bother to take on the future into account. This leads to overspending as the individual is keener on the idea of getting through the day rather than getting through this life.

The sense of responsibility comes with creating a savings account. However, it can also lead to creating a false sense of security in people that lead them to spend more than they can afford at the given moment in time. We tend to forget that we had created a savings account in the first place as a safety net to help us get through a financial crisis. If an individual is constantly using the money in their savings account for unnecessary purchases, then they are not using it correctly. Changing this behavior can be difficult, but keeping the bigger picture in perspective can help an individual forego making such useless purchases.

Creating room in budgets allows an individual to spend their money in discrete amounts. The money saved in the savings account should only be used for true emergencies. Having a thought-out plan in the first place can effectively reduce overspending.

Treat Yourself

The younger generation these days tend to use the term 'Treat Yourself' fearlessly to invoke spending more money on pampering oneself for temporary satisfaction. They do not realize how harmful this behavior can be and lead to a disastrous, and most probably, a bankrupt future. As humans, we tend to fall into the system of rewarding ourselves with an object of our desires as a reward for working hard in life.

We tend to spend too frequently to reward ourselves with the gift, and our willpower is to be blamed for it. People often trick themselves into thinking that they deserve a reward whenever they are able to demonstrate a degree of willpower in their lives. This is only because we view willpower as a limited resource. As a result, overspending on random and unnecessary purchases becomes the norm for them, and they develop an unhealthy habit of splurging to fulfill their desires as a reward. Treating yourself with rewards is not an unhealthy habit, but it is necessary to come up with rewards that require less spending. Developing a healthier habit is the key to reward ourselves without spending too much on unnecessary purchases.

Another way to tackle this problem can be done by simply planning a purchase ahead of time. Instead of resorting to using the savings accounts, we should simply know how much the item costs ahead of time so we can save accordingly during that particular month. It is imperative to make sure that the reward itself has a purpose and is meaningful. Scaling expenses can also help in saving more. For example, try to limit the expense of dining out or shopping once or twice a week to save more.

Home Equity

Spending more money on assets such as property has become normal. People believe that conquering assets contribute more to spending power, making them feel wealthier and financially stable. However, it only helps in adding a false sense of security as you tap into your savings account for home equity. Treating houses like a piggy bank only leads to more unnecessary loans. Borrowing money for gratuitous luxuries leads to unnecessary purchases and place a strain on the family's financial security. Every loan comes with closing costs and charges if an individual fails to repay the debt.

Retirement Plans

It is roughly estimated that around 74% of American citizens do not have a retirement plan set out for themselves according to data collected from survey responses from J.P Morgan Asset Management and Census Bureau. Retirement plans vary from person to person, but a general rule of saving about 80% of pre-retirement salary should be saved as well as income from Social Security, other savings and pensions as well.

It is critical for an individual to consider the average life expectancy and invest time as they might need an income longer than they believe. The cost of care is generally more than what most families expect in their lives. Another reason for the lack of retirement plans is that people are not saving enough. Individuals should save enough so that their retirement income will be around 80% of their pre-retirement and social security income. The main goal is to keep your standard of lifestyle the same way while you were working. The only thing worse than dying is out-living your money. Instead, they spend more than they earn on unnecessary objects to fulfill their wishes. This world runs on the rule of one-size-fits-nobody. The truth is that an average American does not have enough time on their hands to think about their future as they are trying to make it through their current problems.

We are bankrupt in terms of time as we try to do as much as we can in our lives without realizing that retirement costs are higher than what we usually anticipate. An average American believes that they have enough time to save and prolong in making retirement plans. Waiting too long to save can prove to be hazardous for the future.

Every American citizen holds the same fear regarding retirement, i.e., they will always outlive their money. People in America only save up to 5% of their salary; meanwhile, people in Japan save up to 10% of their income every month. This information is not to make you an economist, for the topic of retirement is a far diverse and deeply discussed topic. The main point is to provide practical ideas on how to take control of your life financially. It is crucial to make money your servant, not your master. The first rule of financial independence is to pay yourself first. It is the most critical process of controlling your life financially. An individual should always emphasize on paying themselves first regardless of how selfish it might seem to any outsider.

We are firstly responsible for ourselves. Decide on what percentage of your income you want to save for yourself. Relying on the government to cover our expenses takes that freedom away from us. The more the government takes care of our needs, the less efficient our country becomes. The more government controls us, the less freedom we have.

There are some needs that we cannot ignore, but we should all become self-sufficient so that we do not have to rely more on the government. For many, this fear is more likely to become a reality with the way they are handling their current life. The majority of Americans do not have adequate amounts of savings for their retirement. They cannot support the same form of lifestyle for the rest of their lives. America is currently facing a retirement savings adequacy crisis and is unaware of the major cause behind such behavior.

Keep a Track

It is quite easy for us to judge ourselves for being undisciplined where money is concerned. Modern life is extremely expensive and impossible to live through for some. Money tends to play certain tricks on our minds as emotion comes into play. Whenever we are disturbed by a certain effect, we spend even more to make ourselves feel better about ourselves. However, the feeling of shame soon follows when we realize that we have only made our problems worse.

Spending money is an abstract concept. According to research conducted between people who pay with their credit cards and paper money, those who pay from credit cards tend to lose the sense of money being real. It is easier for them to spend more when using a credit card as compared to using paper money. Studies show that people who spend with hard money tend to feel more hesitancy before making a useless purchase as compared to those using credit cards. Sticking the budget may fail from time to time due to unexpected expenditures regarding home repairs, car repairs, and so on, and such expenditure can greatly affect our lives. Most people are living from paycheck to paycheck, which makes it difficult for them to save more. However, we can overcome this dilemma by cutting back on useless purchases and opt for useful purchases.

It is tricky to spend less and save more, but the fact remains that greater self-esteem is built on self-sufficiency. That comes with saving more and spending less. Keeping a track on ourselves can greatly help us to save more money. By taking advantage of the Hawthorne Effect, we can make our lives easier.

In the 1950s, a researcher named Henry A. Landsberger conducted analysis experiments and came up with the term Hawthorne Effect. It is named after the location where his experiments were conducted from the 1920s to the 1930s. The facility of his research was located in Hawthorne, Illinois, and hence named the term as Hawthorne Effect.

According to the term Hawthorne Effect, humans hold the tendency to work harder and perform better when they are a part of an experiment being conducted by a researcher. Our desire to impress others drives us to work harder and bring changes in our behavior due to the attention we receive from a researcher. This term has been widely discussed in psychology textbooks, especially to those devoted to organizational psychology. Keeping a track on our expenditure can help us realize how much we are spending in a day as compared to how much we earn in a day. For example, if an individual earns $20 USD a day but tends to spend $30 USD a day, then he is earning less and spending more. This way, his/her chances of piling debt is more likely. Similarly, if they spend less than $10 USD, then they will be able to save $10 USD each day. If saving is equal to spending, it can balance their lives easily.

Our mind is the real component that can only push us forward to achieve or overachieve our goals, but sadly, it can also hold us back. Think of money like it is sports. Sports require skills, but it relies heavily on mind games. It takes more will, positive attitude, determination, and commitment to make it to the winning line. Similarly, spending money is just like sports. It takes more willpower and determination to control our spending comparatively. We can blame the economy or the fact we live from paycheck to paycheck, but the truth is that we simply lack financial education.

Most of us did not go through personal finance training and tend to copy the same method we see our parents applying in their lives. We rely on the activities going according to our bearings instead of educating ourselves on how to handle finances properly. This is the reason not much of us know what to do, and most of us are clueless when it comes to money. Ever wondered why that is? It is because most of us fail to acknowledge the importance of keeping our money in check.

We know we need to consume fewer calories and burn more to lose weight, and we know that we need to spend less to save more. But it does not necessarily mean that we follow those rules in our lives just because we know it. Retaining knowledge is futile if we do not have enough willpower to emphasize on the information we have received. We do not follow the guidelines we know about until we have made up our minds.

The majority of people spend more money to keep a certain status in their society. When a person spends more, it means they care more about what others think about them rather than focusing on their future. We spend money on fancy cars, clothes, houses, and several other extravagant items to keep up with the status we have exuded throughout the majority of our lives. It also serves as a self-esteem booster and deludes a person into believing that their status holds more importance over the prospect of going broke. The habit of spending excessively is deeply rooted in insecurity issues as we try to live the life that we cannot actually afford. Spending less money is like pushing a boulder up a hill if we develop the habit of spending more. It is possible to push up the boulder, but it also requires determination and strength to accomplish our goals.

Winning the money game can be a lot of work, but it requires basic steps to control the urges that come with splurging.

Why?

It is crucial to ask why we are spending a certain amount of money. Are we spending money to fulfill a basic necessity, or are we spending money to seek temporary relief? Saving money starts with asking a series of questions that delve deeper into the reasons behind overspending money. This technique involves asking 'Why?' over and over again until you have discovered a deeper reason behind overspending. For example, ask yourself why you need to buy new clothes. Ask yourself if you have enough clothes in the closet. If you are buying clothes just to look good, then ask yourself why that is. If it's to fetch compliments, then you can search for other ways to let people compliment you. It all starts with delving into searching for the true reason behind why and we can utilize it to stop splurging more.

Detouring

Once we uncover the real 'why' behind our spending habits, the more we prioritize our needs against our wants. For example, most people say they want a new mobile, but what they need is an electronic device to keep track of their calls and emails. In short, they want an iPhone, but they need a mobile device. When we discover our needs and the real wants behind our spending habits, then we can take a little detour to discover new ways to get what we want.

The first part of taking a detour in our head is to acknowledge what we want in our life. Guilt factor always makes its way into this line of thinking, but we should do everything in our power to avoid feeling guilty when it comes to buying necessities. It is also great to buy yourself a thing or two to make yourself happy, but we need to do it within a limited budget. Feeling guilty only hinders our journey and is a great demotivating factor. It is in our nature to long for items for fashion purposes, but we need to be careful to control these desires before it controls us.

Keystone Habits

We, humans, exhibit strange behavior without realizing how it is impacting our lives. When a certain bad event occurs, more bad evens tend to follow that certain event. Habits work in the same manner. Once we develop a certain type of habit, other habits are formed naturally without many efforts. For example, a person who is working out and exercising more will tell themselves that they do not eat junk food. They work-out, and soon their lifestyle tends to evolve around that certain habit.

Similarly, people who tend to spend less tend to develop a lifestyle around it. Most of us opt for brand-new things when that same object can be bought at a lower price at a pawnshop. Why is it that we want to buy new books to read when we can simply borrow one from a library or buy it at a lower price from a small, local shop? When we spend more, we tend to buy more brand-new things when that particular item can be purchased at a lower price. It is cause-effective and cost-effective simultaneously. According to Charles Duhigg, these habits are known as Keystone Habit and tend to transform our lives. If the habits are implemented, it will create a ripple effect that can impact our entire life.

In the same manner, we tend to develop the habit of waking up early over the years until it becomes a part of our life, spending less is a habit that can only be formed through years of hard work. Overspending can become a part of our habits, but refraining ourselves involves your will to be made of steel and a mind made up with a resolution.

Spend Carefully

It is crucial to cut down on the expenses that do not impact your life positively and care about it. It can be as big as mortgage planning or something as small as getting coffee on your way to work. Every meaningless expense should be cut down to save more for the future. Saving money can be hard, but it can also lead to having enough to afford things we love and still have money left over.

The main goal of spending less and saving more does not mean we should cut down our expenses completely. We can still buy objects we love and desire while being intentional with the expenditure. It is crucial to fill out the percentage we need first. Do not set the percentage high enough at first as it is difficult to save up at first. It only leads to discouragement and makes us want to give up.

Remember, it is not the amount that matters but rather the regularity of how much you pay yourself daily. The harder we work for our money, the more important it is to set aside a portion from it. Then that money will work hard for you in the long run since a person works hard for years to earn that money.

Remember, temporary relief only leads to long-term grief. Do not allow the money to dictate your life. Instead, dictate the money you spend so that you can lead a comfortable life.

Here I leave you with these quotes that may help you stay more motivated to your money-saving goals:

- Temporary relief long term grief
- The More you have, the more you want.

A man is not rich with what he owns, but he is rich by what he can do without.

Chapter 3 - Part I
Think Constructively

Contrary to popular belief, we spend every waking and sleeping moment of our lives thinking. We either spend the nights thinking about what a crazy day we had, or what went wrong with it, to begin with. We think about what is going to take place tomorrow, or what you plan on doing for the next week. Every decision we make is based on our constructive thoughts.

There are times when we occupy our minds with useless thoughts. We spend more time wondering about what others think of us rather than focusing on our lives. The moment we start caring about what others think about us is the moment when we start losing our own focus. At that given moment, we are wondering about something that does not really affect.

What affects the most is what we think about ourselves, and what we think for ourselves say a lot about us. Thought formations take place long before we start talking in our lives. The question is always about the chicken and the egg.

The real question lies in what came first, our voice, or our thoughts? According to science, our thought formation develops from a tender age of five months. So for everyone who has looked into the sparkling eyes of an infant and wondered what goes on in their fuzzy little head, now you know. Humans form thoughts and display glimmers of consciousness, as well as memory, as early as they are five months old. The subject of consciousness has always been a top priority for neuroscientists.

For decades, they have been searching for an unmistakable signal of consciousness in humans from an early age. It is determined through electrical brain activity. A sign as small as a spark in the cortex of the brain can determine whether the person is minimally conscious when they are under anesthesia. The tests have also been carried out in babies to see whether they are conscious of their surroundings.

The thoughts babies form are obviously different from an adult, but the fact remains that our thinking process has always been a part of us, contrary to popular belief. Whenever we plan on going somewhere, we always think about the right clothes to wear or the events that will take place. Can you imagine yourself showing up in khakis and a t-shirt to someone's wedding? Or going to a BBQ event in your best tux or dress? The way we think matters the most. Whenever we see someone acting out in a strange manner, we automatically assume that they are 'out of their minds,' and the truth cannot be farther from fiction.

We spend every minute of our lives thinking about what to wear, what to do, and how to tackle certain situations in life. Every waking moment of our lives depends on our decision-making – which involves thinking clearly. But before we can jump into that bandwagon, we need to tackle this question:

What is Constructive Thinking?

It is crucial to understand what kind of roles our emotions play to understand what constructive thinking really is. Most people in this world, if not all, commonly believe that emotions make us react to certain circumstances. It is widely believed that emotions are directly related to our actions. Emotions are supposedly a dependent factor in what takes place in the surrounding. An event is believed to trigger people's emotions. This is one of the reasons why people widely believe that they do not have any control over their emotions. They believe that they cannot control the ways in which they express them. Mostly, they believe that there is no way they can actually stop their emotions from occurring in the first place. If that is true, then why is it that people react so differently when they face a similar situation in life? For instance, when people are treated in an unfair manner, they tend to lash out with anger. Once they are consumed with anger, they can actually decide whether they should act on it or not.

The first thing they think is, *"Will it benefit me if I make a showcase out of my anger?"* The first thing that should pop into the person's mind is how their actions will affect them. What we do not realize is that emotions are affected by the manner in which they perceive the circumstance and not the circumstance itself. Perhaps the situation might seem unfair in the way they believe they are treated. Perhaps the way the news was conveyed seemed unfair to them.

Regardless of the situation, anger was invoked in what they believed in and not on what actually took place. There is a line, a fine line, between disappointment and anger, hurt and hate, bitterness, and blame. It can prove to be fatal once it is crossed. If you are near the line and are considering to cross it – as we often do when we believe that we have nothing left to lose - then let me warn you that crossing these lines will not do you any good. Let me warn you not to cross it. Whenever you find yourself standing between these lines, then all you need to do is step back and ask yourself, *"How long am I going to pay for my disappointments? How much more time am I going to waste to nurse my wounds?"* The thing is, it is natural for us to feel anger and hurt whenever someone does anything to hurt us. It is crucial for us to remember that when someone hurts you,

- Don't curse it
- Don't rehearse it
- Don't Nurse it
- But reverse it

Matthew 5:9, 38 to *40*

At some point in our lives, we have to move on. At some point, we have to heal, and we can only move on when we stop repeating the scenario in our head over and over again. The greatest example we can follow and learn from is the example of Jesus. There were times when he was disappointed and hurt throughout his journey in life. Jesus knows what we may be going through because He experienced everything we have and took it to the cross and said, *"Father forgive them for they know not what they do. Jesus Keep Me Near the Cross!"*

Matthew 5:9 New International Version (***NIV***)

"Blessed are the peacemakers for they will be called children of God."

Whenever someone hurts you or does anything to hurt your pride, it is better to forgive them than to hold onto it. That is one of the secrets for leading a peaceful life.

"You have heard that it was said, 'Eye for eye, and tooth for tooth.'[a] 39 But I tell you, do not resist an evil person. If anyone slaps you on the right cheek, turn to them the other cheek also. And if anyone wants to sue you and take your shirt, hand over your coat as well.

In simple words, the crucial key that invokes emotions is perception and not the event itself. We are what we think and what we perceive. The basic foundation of constructive thinking lies here. We become the person we are through the way we perceive the world and the thoughts that are invoked by that perception.

That is why we are a product of our thoughts and not our circumstances. A person who grows up in a deprived environment can still reach great heights if they change their perception about the world. The more they complain, the fewer are their chances of reaching success because of the way they view the world.

The more negatively they perceive the world, the harder it gets for them as our thoughts hold the power to sabotage our own lives. If they keep believing that they will forever be stuck in the same system for the rest of their lives, then it is evident that life will not get better. That is why our perception is a crucial element of life. The only way we can make use of our perception is by adapting the concept of thinking constructive thinking.

Constructive thinking should be viewed as what we perceive the world to be around us rather than what is done to us. Instead of reacting to events that occur in our lives from time to time, the first thing we should focus on is our interpretation and perception. Perceptions are the key to the formation of constructive thoughts as it holds the power to influence our emotions. Emotions are not triggered by our environment, but by our perception, and to control our emotions, we need to change the way we perceive events in life. The biggest mistake we make is by believing in the fact that our emotions come before our thoughts. We believe that feelings come before our thoughts, but that is not true. As stated above, the thoughts invoke our emotions and not the other way around. We form aggressive thoughts whenever we grow angry. Similarly, we develop pessimistic thinking when we are under the influence of sadness or on the slight spectrum of depression.

We start perceiving the world in a negative light after the thoughts are formed. Although it is evident enough that our feelings do affect our thinking process, but the reality of the world is that our thoughts shape our feelings, to begin with. The distinction between the thoughts preceding emotions or emotions preceding thoughts can be easily made on one simple fact.

The former is more conscious while the latter is more preconscious. We have more control over the thoughts that are formed before our emotions are invoked than on the thoughts invoked after our emotions. This is where constructive thinking plays a vital role in our lives. Either you act on that anger and ruin your relationship with the person, or you think carefully with a cool head to prevent it from affecting you. The choice is truly ours if we think about this rationally. We are more aware of our conscious as compared to our pre-conscious existence. This is why we perceive most of the things falsely. It takes more than just understanding what constructive thinking really is to incorporate it into our lives.

This just raises the next question:

What Are Perceptions?

Perception is everything we think, on autopilot. These thoughts enter our minds automatically in cases that we will not even be aware of. Despite everything, perceptions are still thoughts. Here is a perfect example. Imagine you are walking down a busy street in the city. All of a sudden, you feel someone shoves you away or elbows you in the arm.

The chances of you becoming angry depend on how you interpret or perceive the situation. If you perceive that it is done accidentally, you are more likely to act reserved and move on. However, if you believe it to be done deliberately, then you are more likely to pull that person aside and fight it out.

In essence, the event that took place is the same as if someone has shoved you in the elbow. The difference is how you perceive the situation and then decide to act on that particular situation. The automatic thought you have in that very moment, where you are more likely to pass it off as an accident, is known as perception. This perception of yours controls the way you would emotionally react to the event in the next few seconds. Some would argue that one of these perceptions of it being deliberate is right, while others will believe that it was done accidentally. What you think at this very moment will tell you more about yourself than you can think.

While it may be correct for some scenarios, we mostly encounter situations in life that are ambiguous. We will always see the glass being half-empty or half-full. What matters is how we decide to view it and perceive the ambiguous situation that allows you to act in a manner on the basis of good judgment. The more you see the glass being half-full, the chances of becoming happier get higher.

Because those who view the glass being half-full are the ones who practice constructive thinking in their lives.

They maintain a good perception of the events that occur in their lives. According to the emotional intelligence field, there are two types of minds in this world. The one that has wisdom associated with the mind, and the other with a more rational mind.

How can we implement constructive thinking in our life?

The truth is that we emphasize more on our IQ, which is our intelligent quotient, rather than on our EQ, which is our emotional quotient. The problem is that we believe knowledge is power, but the truth is that wisdom is the key. The only way we can perceive wisdom is by taking care of our emotions. It is not necessary to view power in a positive light. Having knowledge of murdering someone is still going to be viewed as negative.

Compassion, empathy, and sympathy is the only thing that holds the knowledgeable person back from committing it. While IQ has its own merits and plays a crucial role in our society, we need to focus on our EQ as well.

Knowledge has its own limitations as well, and these limitations are not properly addressed either. There are many abilities we need to conquer in our lives to live happily. Researchers and experts on Emotional Evaluation believe that constructive thinking is one of the reasons that help us to lead a happier and fulfilling life. The foundation for a much more effective way of thinking has been laid down by the Emotional Intelligence.

To think more constructively, we need to build up our EQ.

- Wisdom is about knowledge using its head
- As you wander through life, no matter where you go, keep your eye upon the donut and not on the hole.
- There is no duty we underrate so much as the duty of being happy.
- It's not the position, but the disposition that makes a man   effective.

Chapter 3 - Part II
How to Build Emotional Quotient

Factual knowledge is beneficial for every individual in the world. It is true that a person cannot do anything in their lives if they do not know how to do it. However, it is crucial to be wise enough to know when to implement your knowledge. That wise part arises with our emotional quotient. EQ, also known as emotional intelligence, is defined as the ability of an individual to identify and manage their own emotions as well as the emotions of other people.

EQ is more than just being capable of identifying our own emotions and being emotionally aware of ourselves. It also includes the ability to explore those emotions and implement them on daily tasks whenever you are thinking critically or solving a problem. The most difficult part comes with managing the emotions of those around you as well as regulating your own emotions when necessary. Emotional intelligence does not have any psychometric scale, unlike general intelligence factor, or IQ, that comes with a validated psychometric test and scale. We cannot simply test out our EQ as easily as our IQ as our emotions completely depend on our 'mood' which progresses as we grow older. IQ is an inborn skill and can be honed accordingly but to a certain limit as compared to EQ, which improves as we go through different stages of our lives. It is evident enough that EQ is criticized on a daily basis among the general public. However, there is a wider appeal within certain sectors of the organization regarding Emotional Intelligence.

Many employees incorporate their emotional intelligence tests into their interview processes or applications. There are many organizations that widely believe that people with emotional intelligence tend to make a better leader and a co-worker. According to some researchers, there is no correlation between Emotional Intelligence and job performance, while others believe that there is a strong link between these two certain fields. The lack of a psychometric scale makes it quite difficult to determine and give a confirmed answer to whether one can predict someone's emotional intelligence or response in any aspect of life. The only way we can determine whether an individual possesses a high EQ level is by observing their signs.

An individual who is highly conscious of their own emotional states and is able to recognize when they are frustrated, sad, or something more subtle is emotionally more intelligent than individuals who feel 'numb' as they are unable to identify what they are feeling. Highly Emotionally Intelligent people are also easily affected by the emotions exhibited by those around them. They are prone to sympathize on a greater level with people and are often viewed as 'sensitive' by others.

There are many ways to hone Emotional Intelligence, but some of the commonly used methods are stated as follows:

Focus on 'Now'

Sometimes, we tend to worry about our future and what it has in store for us. We scare ourselves to the point where we become cautious with every decision we make. Being cautious is not a bad thing per se, but caution often leads to paranoia, and it holds the tendency to ruin better opportunities that are in store for us by ruining it. It is crucial for us to focus on the tasks at hand rather than worrying about the future. Whenever our emotions go haywire, it becomes too difficult to focus on the current task at hand, and it tends to ruin our progress as well. The more we learn on how to control our emotions, the better we will be able to perform our task at hand by focusing on our current present.

Out of Control

People with high Emotional Intelligence do not let anything affect them no matter how negative a certain situation is. Most of the situations we encounter in our lives are out of our control, and there is no point in pondering over them. We cannot control every aspect of our lives, and people with high EQ are aware of this fact. As long as a certain situation is out of their control, they do not let it affect their mood. It is obvious that we cannot control our initial reaction to the situation and end up being upset for a short period of time.

However, there are many people who tend to ponder over it and allow it to affect their lives greatly. The initial reaction to some shocking event is not easy to control, but it is imperative to keep in mind that pondering over the situation for a long period of time is not going to help us in any way. Negative events can only leave an adverse impact on our lives only if we allow it to affect us. Our emotions are made up of the reactions we give to a certain situation. Life gets easier when you learn the fact that there are some events that will always be out of your control. The only thing we can do is wait for it to pass until it no longer affects our life anymore, or we could work towards the betterment with a solution instead.

Accept Failures

As intelligent beings, it is unacceptable for us to face any sort of failures in our life. We have been trained from a very young age to not fail in anything in life. From grades to a soccer game, we are trained to succeed because failure is viewed negatively in every society. Why is failure considered to be one of the worst things to happen in this world? We believe that failing is embarrassing and can ruin your public image.

Contrary to popular belief, failure does not indicate how worthy you are in this world. We all stumble and fail in life from time to time. We might fail a paper, a class, a project, a business, but every failure comes with a lesson. There are people in this world who swear to never go for the same plan if they fail once. Wiser people, on the other hand, go for the same plan but use a different approach to succeed. They apply every sort of methodology and learn to apply the ones that seem better. That is how most of the successful organizations are built around the world. We would never be able to progress this far in life if we had not failed over and over again. Instead of fearing failure, we should train ourselves to accept it as it is an integral part of our life. It is a crucial part of the learning process. The more we fail in a certain field, the more we learn, and what we learn can later be applied as our knowledge when we go through several trials.

Challenge Accepted

Individuals exhibiting high EQ tend to accept challenges without thinking twice. They are the ultimate risk-takers who accept challenges that are out of their comfort zone. A person can only grow professionally and personally when they step outside of their comfort zone. The more secure you feel in life, the more potential you hold in exploring the options lying outside that sense of security. Taking risks can take an individual to greater heights, and every person with high EQ is aware of that fact.

Let go of 'What if'

Every event in life comes with an opportunity for us. But most of us tend to ruin our own opportunity by falling into that 'what if' loop where we can come up with every possible negative aspect in life. We are sometimes only left pondering instead of exploring our 'what if's.' Every 'what if' holds the potential of ruining opportunities for us. We are easily scared of going out of our comfort zone, and instead, we comfort ourselves by bringing up scenarios in our heads that are not likely to happen in our lives. Individuals with high EQ do not waste their time worrying about the what-if scenarios and are ultimate risk-takers. They rely more on 'what is' rather than 'what if,' and that is all that it takes to encourage them to take risks fearlessly.

There are many fields in which Constructive Thinking can come in handy. It takes more than just knowledge to think constructively. It takes wisdom to implement your thinking in real life. The truth is that our mind can only achieve what it can conceive and believe. The more we tell ourselves that we can accomplish a certain task, the more capable we become and accomplish those tasks in life with utmost proficiency.

Here I leave you with these quotes that may help you with adapting critical thinking in life:

- Wisdom is about knowledge using its head
- As you wander through life, no matter where you go, keep your eye upon the donut and not on the hole.
- There is no duty we underrate so much as the duty of being happy.

It's not the position, but the disposition that makes a man effective.

What the mind can conceive and believe, the mind can achieve.

Chapter 4
Creating A Yielding Disposition

A wise man once said that humans are social animals, and it was stated quite correctly. According to Aristotle, humans who decide to shun society from their lives are either gods or beasts. As primitive beings, we simply cannot stand the idea of being alone. Some people, by nature, tend to like being alone, but a person can only go on alone so far before they start craving human affection and company.

As humans, we are naturally oriented toward other people due to our nature. We are biologically programmed to feel more insecure, vulnerable, and alienated whenever we are out alone in a certain public space or personal space. The case might be different for every individual, but it is not easy to suppress the sense of vulnerability that comes with being alone, no matter how strong-willed or hard-headed you are. Living together harmoniously gave rise to making tribes, and through evolution, we formed societies to feel a sense of belonging.

According to Aristotle, the father of philosophy, the truth of things such as the Meta behind the physics is always derived through a logical deduction. The knowledge that we gain from observation is critical but also secondary to the derived principles. It is obvious that a principle is regarded as senseless if the observation contradicts reason. The concept of logic was coined by Aristotle, who observed that logic is one of the most important systematic toolsets for decision-making processes.

He gave the reason why societies are formed. Societies are formed based on a specific part of the culture, ideas, customs, and social behavior that form the basis of families, the global economy, and the government of our country. It was a gradually slow process that evolved over the period of time as tribes became larger and larger before they evolved into a larger group of people.

Today, these groups of people who live together in a particular area are known as a society. There are many reasons why we tend to form our own society. It helps us feel secure and closer to someone else who shares the same interests as us. Being social is also one of the many ways to create connections in life that might help us in the future.

There are many advantages that come with living in a society as it shapes our thoughts, our likings, and our behavior for better or for worse. It all depends on what kind of a society we are willing to create and live in.

As social beings, we are opinionated about topics that might be simple or controversial. We are the only primal creatures who are capable of talking and communicating through words rather than actions. As compared to humans, other primates are only capable of producing vocalization of a limited range. We use our unlimited range of vocalization to communicate with each other and to create a better understanding.

However, we also use our ability to spark conversations that transform into two of the following things:

- Debate
- Argument

Our nature of talking tells us a lot more about our personality and gives a hint toward the background we have all been raised in. Our nature is revealed through the behavior we exhibit within our societies. It is an indicative factor of who we are as people. Every conversation holds the potential of turning sour the moment controversial topics around the world are discussed on a platform. Whether it is a bigger platform, or a smaller one, these two things hold the power to change a person's opinion for better or for worse. We have all heard the phrase, *"Sticks and stones may break my bones, but words will never hurt me."* As overrated as this quote might be, the truth is that our words hold the power to do more damage than we can imagine.

Words can leave an emotional scar that can never be healed over a period of time. Physical damage can be healed and forgotten, but it takes real strength to heal emotionally. Once a person starts believing in other's words, it holds the potential of scarring, hurting, and leaving wounds on a person's soul.

Our words hold the power to transform a person into a better version of themselves, but it also holds the power to completely destroy someone. It all depends on how we choose to utilize the power that comes with our words. Difference between Argument and Debate Not many people are able to differentiate between arguments and debates. For all we know, both are nouns that involve a conversation taking place between two or more people.

We convey our thoughts, feelings, and knowledge through these conversations to create, for the lack of better words, a good understanding. The only difference between these two words is the utilization, connotation, or a hidden meaning underlying the tone behind every word.

We all tend to argue with people every once in a while due to our nature of being opinionated. Arguments involve statements that either speak in favor of a certain topic or against it. Arguments are commonly used in the court of law to provide facts as well as evidence to persuade the jury. The only difference is that they hold the discussion in a formal environment, and each lawyer is allotted a certain limited time to get their points across to the judge.

Most of the time, we argue with other people out of anger or during a heated situation. There are other factors that contribute to sparked arguments that take place in our lives. We might argue due to lack of sleep, or simply for having a bad day. However, most of the arguments are also backed up with rational responses that make a person feel the need to prove others wrong in the given conversation. Arguing with other people only lands us in a vicious and into a never-ending cycle.

Every argument gives rise to another argument that only goes on and on until the speakers tire themselves out or are simply fed up with each other. The only reason why we continue our argument is that we feel that our points are not getting across to the other person or that we are being proven wrong by the other participant. Most of the time, we tend to argue on topics we are not well-versed that can lead to a bigger conflict. Such arguments also hold the potential of embarrassing us when the other speaker thrusts hard facts on our face.

Types of Arguments

According to researchers, there are three types of arguments that take place on any platform; in our professional or personal aspects of life.

Deductive Argumentation

Deductive argumentations arise from reasoning done on premises that are presented. These arguments rely on factual information that leads to a valid conclusion. For example, deductions are based on reasoning and facts. The easiest way to explain deductive argumentation can be done through the following example.

If X is Y and Y is Z, then X is also equal to Z.

This type of argumentation was first proposed by Aristotle under the nomenclature of 'syllogism.' However, there is a certain limitation to deductive argumentation due to the lack of exhaustive evidence.

Inductive Argumentation

Due to the lack of exhaustive evidence, it is necessary to rely on other entities, and that is done through inductive argumentation. These arguments are created to support the conclusions that are created by deductive argumentation. They solely arise to confirm whether the conclusions derived from deductive arguments are correct or wrong.

Using the same example as stated above, we can explore the areas of why we believe that X is equal to Z.

The answer would revolve around the fact that X is Y, and Y is Z, so it automatically means that X is also equal to

Z. This kind of argument is also useful in supporting our theories and our interpretation of things.

Abductive Argumentation

Abductive Arguments explore the same premises as Inductive Argumentation with the exception that they provide the best explanation for the conclusion that is presented from Deductive Argumentation. It helps us by providing the best logical explanation. It provides the simplest reasoning for a given set of observations.

These types of argumentation can also be applied in our personal lives when we argue with other people. Our arguments may be related to something as insignificant as telling someone to get something for you. Or it can be as big as arguing about who should be nominated as the next team leader within a professional environment. These arguments escalate at a rapid state, the more we carry on with them. Soon, these arguments are transformed into screaming sessions that leave both speakers and parties unsatisfied and unhappy.

At the end of every argument, we notice how each party tries hard to prove who is wrong and who is right. As primal creatures, we do not like admitting the fact that we were in the wrong. We believe accepting defeat will only humiliate us further, and none of us can accept that.

We want to prove to others that we are always right because we cannot bring ourselves to admit that we were in the wrong all along. In the current era, we see the youth raising their voice against many injustices going around in the world. They raise their voice for awareness since they do not want to repeat the same mistakes made by the older generations. The youth of every country plays a crucial role in developing a country into a better state. Raising healthy debates on social media can help create more awareness as compared to arguing about it. Arguing is only healthy to a certain limit as long as it remains within the boundary of a debate.

Why are debates better?

The only reason why any discussion ends up becoming an argument is due to the hostility exhibited by both speakers. It may be as simple as an eye-roll, clicking of the tongue, or a certain dirty look that can trigger the other party and turn the situation uglier by the second. The moment one of the speakers raises their voice is the moment when an argument is initiated. The only way we can debate is by opening up our minds.

Being Open-Minded

More often than not, it seems impossible to accept or change our own opinions regarding a certain topic. For example, the topic of feminism is on the rise, and there are two parties; the ones who support the concept of liberating women and the ones who are against their liberation and equality. There are many factors that lie within your mindset, which tells you why you should be pro-feminist or anti-feminist. You support the idea or go against it due to your own perception.

Changing perception is not easy either as we perceive things we have been taught to observe from a very young age. They say every child is a reflection of their parents until they gradually evolve into their own type. Similarly, most of our ideals and ideas have been drilled into us from a very young age. That is why we feel a great sense of aversion whenever someone presents an ideology that goes against yours.

Opening up your mind and broadening your perception is the perfect way to tackle this sense of aversion. Most of the problems in our life arise due to our own close-mindedness than the actual problem we face. It is imperative to have an open mind when you are presented with a controversial topic discussion or a general discussion that goes against your ideologies. We can turn any argument into a constructive argument by opening up ourselves to different ideas and prospects being presented at the given moment. We are always so busy trying to prove ourselves right that we often overhear the valid argument the other party is presenting. We talk more and hear less. This just creates another set of problems for us and turn the argument more heated.

The process to become an open-minded person is not that easy as it takes us beyond our comfort zone. We are forced to accept the fact that some of the beliefs and values we had been taught as a child were all a farce to enforce a controlling environment. Throughout our lives, we always tend to surround ourselves with those who share the same thinking and beliefs as us.

We are unable to 'fit in' with those who do not share the same view and beliefs because of the contradictory discussions that pop up one after another. Surrounding ourselves with people who share the same ideologies only prevents us from becoming open-minded. The moment we interact with someone who is a little different than us is the moment where we actually struggle as their ideas challenge our own. Hence, we prefer to stick with those who are the same as us without realizing that it is doing more harm than it is doing good for us. There are many benefits that come with becoming open-minded. We are more intrigued by other's views and their understanding. It helps us let go of that controlling feeling, as a result of which, we free ourselves from being in control of our own thoughts.

Being receptive to new thoughts and ideas can challenge our current beliefs but also help us gain more knowledge on the topic. Being open-minded can also make you more confident as it helps in creating a strong sense of self. You know that you are no longer confined by your own beliefs, nor are you confined by other's beliefs.

The more you learn about the world around you, and the more you try to understand the people around you, the more you gain confidence as it helps in strengthening your belief in yourself.

However, the only challenge it poses is that we actually have to open up our perception.

Talk Less, Hear Less and Listen More

One of the biggest problems posed by many people is that they have a tendency to talk more and listen less. Humans are also gifted with the sense of hearing, but the only problem is that we hear, but we do not listen. There is a huge difference between hearing someone and actually listening to them. We always overlook the context of the topic that is being discussed so that we can jump in to present our own points within an argument or a debate.

Individuals who are more prone to talking more and listening less can easily lose an argument. Listening to others' opinions and experiences can help us grown into a better person. None of us can become open-minded without listening to others. The more we listen, the more knowledge we gain, and we are more likely to end a discussion on a better note. We can only grow our understanding by listening to the opinions of others so that we can deduce their thinking before we can present our own opinions.

We can easily find common ground with those whose opinions and thoughts differ from our own. As a result, we no longer limit our interaction with those who come from a different belief system. The power of listening can help us progress in life as we become aware of our surroundings. It helps us in reading a certain situation in life that we can utilize for our own benefits. The only reason why we argue is to prove to others that we are always right. However, being right all the time just proves that you have a limited range of knowledge, and everything that proves you to be wrong becomes invalid in your opinion.

Here are some points that can help you create your own yielding disposition:

- There is something wrong if you are the only one in the room who is always right.
- It's easy to be an angel if nobody ruffles your feathers.
- Talk is cheap because supply exceeds the demand.

- A person once said, *"If I agreed with you, we would both be wrong."*

Chapter 5
Be Grateful

From a very young age, we are always taught how we should be grateful in life because others might have it worse than us. Our parents teach us that this is how we should be grateful and this is what we, as parents, might be teaching our kids. The truth is that the true sense of gratefulness is not invoked when we compare ourselves to others.

It is invoked when we look around our surroundings and start counting our blessings without keeping an eye on what others might or might not have. It is an innate response of humans to compare themselves with others. However, comparing ourselves with others can never really bring us a sense of peace or gratefulness.

We mostly use the comparison method as a means to deal with the negative thoughts we have in our lives. The comparison method is a trap we all confine ourselves in. Whenever we want to buy a new shirt, we always tend to pick two before comparing them with each other. We always think about choosing the best one out of two without realizing that there might be better items hidden in the back of the store. That is exactly the kind of method we use when we compare our situation with others. You will always tell yourself that someone out there has worse than you do. This actually affects your mental and physical health negatively rather than producing a permanent solution to your ever-prevailing problem.

The only reason why we tend to feel grateful is that we think 'someone else might have it worse' is because we have been programmed to think this way. We are always taught to look at the brighter side of the things in this world by keeping the darker side in the back of our minds. You do not necessarily need to go through an accident and tell yourselves to endure the pain just because someone has it better.

It is imperative for a person to acknowledge their pain and suffering instead of downplaying it by consoling themselves that others have it worse. Why should we feel obliged to not consider our feelings for that 'someone' who is living in a completely different world than yours? If you are not someone who will compare yourself with others and think, *"I don't have as much as they do,"* while wallowing in feelings of jealousy, pity, and despair, then why are you consoling yourself by telling yourself that others have it worse than you? We are always taught not to compare with each other, but that all changes when we are taking notes of our problems and look back on what we have. The trap of comparison can never truly satisfy you, and you need to learn how to respond positively to every adversary you are faced with in this life. Do not fall into the trap where you are taught to be grateful just because someone else has it worse than you. Learn how to be grateful because you truly appreciate the life you have acquired for yourself.

The Art of Being Grateful

Being grateful for what we have in this life is a form of art itself. The art of being grateful is not easy to master, but the good news is that you do not have to be talented to be good at it. An individual expresses their feeling of gratitude in numerous ways. Before jumping into the feeling itself, we should first understand what the word 'grateful' means. We know the dictionary definition of this word, but very few of us are aware of this word's origin. Knowing about the word's origins can also help us grasp the true concept that had been utilized before its emergence. The word 'gratitude' translates into 'grace,' 'graciousness' or 'gratefulness.' Gratefulness is an expression of appreciation for what we have in the world. This word might hold a different meaning for individuals. Some might believe that we should be grateful when we receive something, and some might believe that we should be grateful when we do something in life. However, this expression does not have to be bound by our limited imagination. We can simply be grateful for waking up to live another day. We can be grateful for the good weather or simply for the fact that we get to experience life for another day.

The real problem is that we are always so busy with everything going on around in our lives that we forget to take a moment out to appreciate it. For example, let's suppose you go out to work every day. You get into your car or your bike with a clear destination in your mind. You are so focused on taking the routes with the least traffic that you forget to do not pay attention to everything going on around you. You are focused on making it to work on time because you do not want to check in late. Thousands of thoughts are running through your mind that you forget to appreciate the fact that you have a means through which you can travel. You barely notice how clear the skies look, or how you woke up with great health today. This is just one of the many examples of how we are so absorbed in our lives that we do not think about taking a moment out of our hectic schedule to appreciate the fact that we are still breathing today. The hectic schedule always keeps us on our toes that we do not bother to be grateful for anything.

What is the point of living a life where we do not take our time to appreciate all the good and the bad things going on in our lives? Yes, you read that right. We should not only focus on just being grateful for the good things in our lives. Those things that have adversaries in our lives can teach us lessons we would not have ever learned otherwise. Every adversary in our lives has a purpose and a lesson attached to it.

These lessons teach us not to repeat the same mistakes we tend to keep making in our lives. Today, we are all so busy trying to stay ahead of others that we forget to ask ourselves who we are trying to outrun here in this world. Who are we exactly competing against here? Are we competing against others? Or are we just trying to compete against time? What is our purpose in this world? Why were we brought here? These questions can only be answered when you look deep into yourself and try to find your inner person. We all have different versions of ourselves. We display a different behavior when we are surrounded by certain groups of people. The truth is that we have different versions of ourselves locked inside of us. These versions are only brought out whenever we face a certain situation in life.

For example, the behavior you exhibit around your boss may be different from the behavior you exhibit around your colleagues. The reasoning behind this methodology of behavior may be obvious, but the truth is that sometimes we tend to forget who we really are when we get used to this trope.

In order to be grateful in life, you need to know who you are as a person and what you need to do to be happy in this world. You need to know your inner-self before you move onto taking the first step of practicing gratefulness in life. Before you can start practicing the art of being grateful, you need to ask yourself why you want to do it. Are you doing it because someone else is telling you to do it? Or are you doing it because you are tired of wallowing in self-pity? Are you doing it for yourself, or are you doing it for others? If you are doing it for others, then there is no point in taking the initiative at all. Only because you will find yourself falling back into the same trap if you do this for other's sake. You need to practice this trait for your own self. It will always help you push through the toughest phase of life as well. It is impossible to avoid the feeling of self-pity. As humans, we tend to fail at certain points in our lives, and this failure invokes a sense of self-pity. We ask ourselves all sorts of questions when we go through this phase in life.

We always ask ourselves, *"Why me? Why is this happening to me? It could happen to anyone, yet it happened to me. What am I doing wrong in life?"* These thoughts only negatively impact our health and worsen the situation by placing us in a wrong sense of victim-complex. The only way we can battle our thoughts of self-pity is by practicing the art of gratefulness in the world.

Once you realize that you want to practice gratefulness for your own sake, then you have already taken the first step of trying to master this art. We do not need to go through amazing experiences in our lives just to be grateful. Most of us can simply be grateful for being well and alive in the world. We should be grateful for being a part of this world that has so much to offer us. There are so many possibilities out there waiting for us, and yet, we tend to stop our own progress in life by wasting our time by wallowing in self-pity. Do not look at others and console yourself that others have it worse. If you do so, only then will you start focusing your shift on those who also have it better than you. It is imperative that you avoid overthinking at all costs.

The only thing you need to focus on is yourself. Sometimes you need to look at yourself and simply be grateful for being well and alive. Even if you are sick or have an illness, be grateful because it reminds you that we took our health for granted when we were so well. A lot of us are grateful to simply breathe after we get through the flu. We complain about having a blocked nose and stuffy face for weeks as we go through our sickness.

The moment we take our first breath after we get well is a feeling we cannot simply explain in words. It feels much better when you take a breath of fresh air. This is exactly the kind of response gratefulness will invoke inside of you the moment you start practicing in your life.

How to be Grateful?

There is no proper way to practice gratefulness. We cannot simply look for one way to practice this art. This feeling of gratitude comes from within. It is an emotion that is invoked on its own. That's how powerful the emotion of gratitude really is. It holds the power to turn your upside down world into a proper direction. However, there are simple ways through which you can practice gratefulness in your life.

Smile More Often

Most people associate the act of smiling in public as a mindless act. We go through so many dreary faces in the street that we start adopting one ourselves so that we do not stand out. Smiling more often can make you more inviting, and it can also trigger the happy hormones in your mind. Just the general act of smiling can help rewire your brain and trick it into thinking that you are happy. The feeling of happiness will also help you feel more grateful for everything going on around you.

Notice Your Surroundings

The more you notice your surroundings, the more grateful you will feel. The perfect beauty of nature can help you soothe your mind. You can either spend your time worrying about something that can be done at home while taking a walk through the park. Or you can simply catch a break from your inner monologue and take in the beauty of the nature surrounding you. It can be as small as a lone flower growing on the side of the road, or it can be as vast as the blanket of the sky over your head. The more you spend time with nature, the grateful you will be for having the ability to see that beauty with your own eyes.

Appreciate Those Around You

It is imperative to take some time out of your schedule to let others know how much they really mean to you. Not only will it help you feel grateful for having such wonderful people in your life, but it will also make them feel grateful to have someone like you in their lives. From a little 'I love you' to 'I appreciate having someone like you in my life,' you can watch them smile back at you with wonder in their eyes. Appreciation is the most important factor in keeping human relationships intact. Practicing it on a daily basis can help you feel great about yourself as well. You will feel lucky to have so many people to appreciate in life.

Push Away Negative Thoughts

This might be the toughest category in the world. We cannot simply train ourselves to not let the negative thoughts pop into our heads. Try as you all might, there are some moments in life that will make you think negatively. Thoughts are a product of the events taking around us. Whenever a negative thought pops up into your mind, immediately retract that thought back and counter it with a positive thought.

You can either keep focusing on why you think your life is ruined. Or you can think about solutions for your problem instead of simply wallowing in self-pity. The moment you take every adversary in life as a challenge, your life changes tremendously. Pushing away negative thoughts can help us focus on positive ones.

Meditate

Meditation does not necessarily mean pulling out your yoga mat and practicing breathing techniques. Meditation can be something as simple as lying down in bed after a long day. You can simply close your eyes, and recount your entire in your head. The more you think about your day, the more you realize where you made mistakes in your life while you can also recount the fun you had throughout the entire day. Meditation can help you realize how blessed you really are to be alive as it calms you down to your core.

Help Others

We all know how hard it is to ask for help. We cannot simply ask a stranger to help us with whatever problem we face in the streets. That is why it is important for us to help those who are struggling tremendously. It is not necessary for you to help those you know. You can also help those who are too afraid to ask for it. For example, if you see someone having trouble carrying so many grocery bags in their arms, offer them some assistance. Or you could just hold onto the elevator doors when you see someone running towards it. Helping others is an act of kindness that comes with a ripple effect. The kindness you show to someone today will go onto show the same act of kindness to others. When you help others, you create a sense of obligation for them to help others next time. You should always be grateful for the fact that you are in a position to help others. By   following these basic steps of simply appreciating your life, you will easily find yourself being grateful for being in good health.

If you think you do not have a good life, then try to change your train of thoughts and watch yourself fall in love with life again. Focusing on your strengths rather than focusing on your weaknesses will also make you feel grateful for being here. Gratitude can help you transform your life completely. It can improve your health, as those who are often grateful for everything they come across in life, experience fewer headaches and pain.

People who practice gratitude also tend to take better care of their health and exercise more often. It also helps you open up new friendships with strangers as they will more likely be attracted by the positive aura you exhibit. It is more likely that you will be able to constitute good manners if you are more grateful in life. Being grateful also rewires your brain psychologically by reducing toxic emotions such as envy, jealousy, and regrets in our minds. Needless to say, it also helps you sleep much better at night. There are many reasons why we should take some time out of our daily routines to thank God. He has commanded us to be grateful because He is aware of how easy it is for mankind to fall into despair over everything he does have in his possession.

"God created everything, and He created it good." - **Timothy 4:4-5**

There is no doubt that everything in this world is completely unique and beautiful. God has taken His time out to create everything for us, so we should take some time out of our lives to thank Him for creating us.

"God made us, and we are His people." -**Psalm 100:3**

This is God's way of saying that He has not created a single man or woman who is full of flaws. This is His way of telling us not to hate ourselves because we are His people, and therefore, we are His valuable subjects in this world.

"Give thanks to the Lord for He is good. His love endures forever." -Ps. 118:29

Thanking Lord is also one of the greatest ways to worship Him. We should always be grateful for the privileges we have been provided with because these privileges are not that easily attainable for some people in the world. Even if you hate your job, you should be grateful that you at least have a job in the first place that can help you support your family or yourself. Gratitude for life also provides you with a feeling of self-sufficiency, and you will never go out of the way to seek love from someone else.

This is one of the many ways you can be grateful for God's grace and eternal salvation. The art of being grateful can also help us redeem ourselves for all of the sins we committed by being ungrateful in our lives.

Sometimes we should just rely on God when things go bad in our lives and be grateful for being in His good graces. Every problem that befalls on us is just another way for Him to test our patience and resilience. He provides us with trials in this life that can help us redeem ourselves and that we should be happy with the fact that we are being provided with a second chance. Because not many people get second chances, and out of everyone in the world – He chose you!

Being grateful can be because of many factors in this world. You should just allow this feeling to become a permanent part of your life. It can help you focus on the gifts you have been provided with in this world rather than complaining about things you do not have in your life.

Here I leave you with these quotes that may help you with adapting the art of being grateful in life:

- Let's not miss out on the joy of what we have because we're obsessed with what we don't have.
- Be not drunk with wine, but with gratefulness.
- Give thanks unto the Lord for He is good. His steadfast love endures forever.
- A forced smile is much better than a sincere frown!
- If you smile a lot, you as you get older, you will have a twinkle in your wrinkle.

I am too blessed to be stressed because: *"God whispers to us in our pleasures, speaks in our consciences, but shouts in our troubles. They are His megaphone to rouse a deaf world."* - **C.S.** **Lewis**

Chapter 6
Rule Your Moods

"It is not what happens to you, but how you react to it that matters."

-Epictetus

Emotions are one of the most complex parts of a human being. It is widely believed that our emotions depend on external factors rather than internal factors. This line of thinking can only make a person act out on their emotions uncontrollably. This type of thinking allows our emotions to overpower us and render us weaker with each passing day. There are some things that are in our control, and then there are some things that are not in our control.

We cannot control the external factors that occur in our daily lives. You cannot control the way other people think about you, or the way they feel about you or the way they treat you. Try as you might, there are just some things that can never be in your control. There are times where all of your efforts go to waste no matter what you do for that specific person in your life. The point is that you cannot control others' actions around you. You cannot even control your own world as every little plan you make for yourself comes with a twist of its own called 'LIFE.' But do you know what you can control in your life? Your emotions. Let us dive into the topic of emotions in detail and see how it holds the power of influencing our lives on a daily basis.

What are Emotions?

The scientific and the basic definition states that our emotions are a set of strong approaches that are derived from an individual's circumstances, mood, or relationships with others. Our emotions are often confused with 'feelings' because these two terminologies are believed to be one of the same. The truth, however, states that emotions are our reaction to external stimuli around us.

It is the physical portrayal of what your mind is experiencing at the moment. Feelings, on the other hand, are a mental portrayal of what your body is experiencing. These two interlinked terminologies are somewhat similar, and yet, they both share different meanings because of how similarly they play out in our minds and bodies. However, emotions and feelings are vastly different from each other.

Emotions are invoked inside of our bodies whenever we experience something good or bad in our lives. It is a reaction to our environment. These emotions are followed by a different range of feelings that help us understand what our mind and body are telling us at the moment. Emotions play a crucial part in the field of the human body, whereas feelings play a crucial part in the field of the mind. The mind and body of a human being are connected in many ways, but emotions and feelings interlink these two different parts of our anatomy in a completely unique way.

Emotions hold a subjective response of how a person reacts to their external stimulus. The physiological response involves a physical reaction to your surroundings. So if you have ever felt butterflies in your stomach before an interview, then it is your body rather than your mind telling you that you are nervous. Feelings will be followed by a mixture of your emotions, triggering fearful thoughts in your mind and will turn your nervousness into anxiousness. Do you notice how these two entities play a similar role and yet produce different results? During the physiological response, it is your body telling you that you are nervous. The shaking of your legs, the trembling in your hands, the crack in your voice, and the palpations of your heart tell your mind that you are nervous. They give a physical response, and hence, it is widely believed that the body is involved during the time your emotions are invoked. After that, your mind takes over as it receives signals from your body and creates a number of thoughts in your head that add more fuel to an already burning fire.

But wait! Not all emotions are bad! Sometimes, our emotions can also lead us to feel a light feeling in our chest. There are times when people claim that they feel too 'high' off their happiness, and that is what our emotions can exactly do! Your body feels as light as a feather and triggers your feelings into a happy one. Everything starts to look better than ever.

Your mind is completely open to all of the possibilities of this world, and you start reacting to everything around you with a smile on your face. You automatically start displaying positive behavior in your life, and that is known as the behavioral response. Our behavioral response plays a major part in our lives as half of the things in our life depend on how we tend to behave with others around us.

However, more often than not, most people also confuse the terms 'emotions' with 'moods.' These terms are used interchangeably, but there are many psychologists who make the distinctions between these two terminologies. These two differ in various ways. An emotion is an intense but short-lived response. For example, if you and your friend have a discussion on the topic of politics, it might end up being a debate, and it might leave you feeling frustrated because you were unable to convey your thoughts properly.

This can ultimately lead to being angry but only for a short while. A mood, on the other hand, is a milder response, but it is longer-lasting as compared to emotions. Moods do not completely depend on an external stimulus. If you have ever felt gloomy for a few days without any clear and identifiable reason, then it simply means you have been dwelling in a bad 'mood' for a while. Moods are long-lasting despite being milder reactions and can lead to long-term effects if the individual does not take proper care.

Control Your Emotions

The truth is that our emotions hold the power of influencing our lives immensely. A person can either live their lives by dwelling in regrets or sorrows, or they can live their lives by adopting a positive attitude. It all depends on how we actually want to live. There are times when people let their emotions get the best of them. Remember, emotions invoke a behavioral response as well and can cause you to act out in unimaginable ways. You will either react positively or negatively. Our behavioral response can vary from person to person as it is also shaped by the kind of society we live in.

For example, if you live in a society that is more expressive about their opinions, then you will inhabit their behavior by observing them closely. It is estimated that Americans are more vocal about everything around them due to their 'freedom of speech' as compared to Asians who view silence as respect. These responses we exhibit also depend on the type of environment we are living in, but there are numerous ways we can change these responses for our own benefits.

It is not easy to control our emotions, but it is not entirely impossible either. The conquest of controlling our emotions started as early as 300 B.C. An ancient Greek Philosophy of Stoicism was developed by Zeno of Citium.

His philosophy explained the concept of self-control and fortitude as the only way to overcome destructive emotions. It is not the process of extinguishing emotions, but rather transforming them into a resolute form of abstinence. The less we focus on the pleasures this world has to offer, the more enabled we become to judge more clearly and remain calm in our lives. Our main purpose is to take an active part in our lives but become less attached to it. Stoicism is the freedom from suffering – which should be the ultimate goal of every person in this world.

Stoicism is not a set of ethical claims or set of beliefs, but rather, it is a way of living our lives while constantly practicing and training ourselves continuously. It is the practical way of living where logic is incorporated in every aspect of life. The philosophy of Stoicism aims to free a person from anguish and suffering through the pursuit of reasoning. The only way we can reason is by detaching ourselves from our emotions and judging everything and everyone around us with a clear mind. Though the word 'stoicism' nowadays means to be completely emotionless, the true sense of the word originated with the philosophy of being indifferent to the world around us as it is not in our control. We can opt to have a passive reaction to external events and act with equanimity (composure) when faced with the highs and lows in this world. People who follow stoicism are known as stoics, and they try to understand the natural universal reason in all things. It allows one to think with a clear and unbiased mind. That is why they believe that ignorance breeds sadness and evil in the world because these people are unaware of their own universal reason.

They do not know why they exist, and that can form deviant thoughts in their minds. The only solution to such unhappiness and evil in the world lies in the philosophy of stoicism. This philosophy also relies on judging your own behavior to determine why you have diverged from your path of universal reason. Hence, stoicism is about living according to nature. By nature, the stoics mean that we should live according to the laws of the universe as well as to the essential nature of our reasons.

Stoicism provides us with the framework of living well in any situation and at any stage of our lives. It helps in reminding us what is truly important in life as well as it provides us with practical strategies to attain more valuable things in life. It is not necessary for you to learn the entirely new lexicon of this philosophy in order to practice stoicism. Many athletes, entrepreneurs, and politicians practice stoicism in their lives as it helps in providing them with inner peace – which is the main objective of every human in this world.

Most of the early stoics came up with the perfect solution to practicing stoicism. Keep in mind that stoicism is the only way of controlling your emotions and not the other way around. It is easy for our emotions to control us due to our own lack of self-control.

Steps to Controlling Emotions

Hone Your Willpower

People with stronger willpower can easily control their emotions as compared to those with weaker willpower. However, our willpower also depends on how we choose to implement it in our daily lives. Whatever happens in our lives is not within our control, but how we choose to react to it is very much in our control. According to Epictetus, a philosopher and a stoic, he believes that a man is not really disturbed by the events that occur in his life but rather by the way he perceives those situations.

The undeniable truth of our life not being in our control is recognized by all stoics. Epictetus had no reason to believe he could control anything because he was born as a slave. His master had permanently crippled him by breaking his leg, and it was widely believed that he would live and die in poverty.

However, Epictetus would always claim that even if his body was not within his control, his desires, opinions, and aversions were still his to control. It was the only thing he owned, and he used this practical thinking to move ahead in his life.

We can learn a great lesson from Epictetus, a philosopher who is well known today. He honed his willpower because it was the only thing in his control, and his thinking transformed his life for the better.

Save Time

Time is one of the greatest assets of human beings. Unlike other material possessions, time is something you can never get back once you lose it. The experiences that you go through in that particular time frame can never be regained no matter what you do. That is why we should strive to save our time rather than wasting it on meaningless things. Stoics believed that time is one of our greatest tools. The way we utilize time says a lot about who we are as people. Those who have more time on their hands are clearly not doing enough in their lives and are simply using it to entertain themselves in one way or another.

Today, the thought of procrastination is idolized by many people in the world. We would rather waste our time than completing a particular task on hand. However, not having time on hand can also negatively affect us. The more we cram our calendars and schedules, the more we are likely to get burned out from our routine and become slaves to our time.

Either way, whichever spectrum you fall into does not matter as long as you understand the importance of time. Only because we should know that time is of the essence, and while we may think we have a lot of time to do whatever we want in the future, we actually do not have time as it is scarce, and the future is unknown.

Stay Focused

It is possible for us all to lose our focus whenever we are confronted with a distraction. Today, we have a lot more work to do than our predecessors did, and we find ourselves being overwhelmed by the number of options we have. Whether it is related to the field of work or vacation spots – we know too much to be able to choose what to do in our lives.

Instead of being distracted by meandering things, it is better to create a list of goals for ourselves so that we remain focused. These distractions can be in various forms. From people to tasks, distractions take on these forms to stop us from reaching our goals. In order to achieve our goals, we need to stay focused and remind ourselves not to be distracted by our emotions or anything else that comes in our way.

Outsourcing Happiness

Most of us have the habit of outsourcing our happiness in different ways. We tell ourselves that our happiness truly lies in the external world around us rather than it being internal. We are happy whenever someone else does something special or amazing for us. Oftentimes, our primal need to be liked and accepted by others also holds the power to make us feel happy. We spend more money than we possess, and we buy things we do not need in this world to impress people who really do not matter much to us. We should value ourselves to the point where we do not lose a sense of 'self' when it comes to pleasing others.

We all want to be liked, but when you trample your self-respect for it, then perhaps it's time for you to stop looking for others' approval. What matters the most – or what should matter the most to us – is our own approval. Yet, we start seeking approval from the outside rather than the inside. This only results in unhappiness and dissatisfaction from both sides. The moment we let go of our needs to please everyone is the moment we start focusing on ourselves.

We make decisions that can help us transform our lives when we stop caring for others' approvals. As long as you approve of your own self, you will no longer need consolidation from others. You will become less likely to be influenced by others. This can help in stopping the habit of outsourcing your own happiness because we all know that happiness comes from within.

Say Good-bye to Ego

Ego is the heart of arrogance. We all think that we know everything in this world – even if it is not particularly true. There will always be some sort of new fact or a new discovery that we will not know about until someone passes on the message to us. Even then, we try to come up with different facts that we know as an act to show that you have the same amount of knowledge as the other person. Ego is the main emotion that makes us feel more adequate than we actually are.

However, the world is not made up of black and white. There are areas of greys because we know that everything we hear is not exactly what is being said. Everything we see is not the truth, but our own perception of what is going on around us. We simply assume everything, and that costs us more than we understand.

Egoistic people also believe that they are better than everyone else around them. They also please people, and that is why stoics toss away their ego as it gives birth to vanity. If we assume that we know everything in this world, then we will be unable to come up with more strategic plans to solve our problems that may show up tomorrow.

Critical thinking can easily be stomped by ego, and we know that we cannot live in this world without applying critical thinking. It is easy for most of us to get frustrated because we are habitual of staying comfortable in our solitude. The evolution of man occurred due to his urge to seeking comfort in life. It has become an integral part of us that we tell ourselves that we cannot live without comfort.

Our encounter with the slightest inconvenience invokes an outrage in us because we are no longer used to minor setbacks. We are easily irritated by the slightest inconvenience we face, and as a result, it makes us feel unhappy. The more we stop focusing on our comfort and learn to live with discomfort, the more we will be able to enjoy our lives happily.

Controlling our emotions can also help us living a better life as it helps us focus on our present rather than our future. Although we should strive for better things in life, we should also learn how to be happy with what we have been blessed with in this world. We have a lot of valuable things in our life, yet we walk on a journey to seek more in order to fill this insatiable desire of possessing everything.

This will only create a never-ending cycle of desires, and the best way to control our desires is to monitor them one by one. Instead of focusing on what you want, you should focus on what you need. If you have everything you need, then what more can you possibly want? Perhaps it is time for us to smile even during the time of our adversaries as it is out of our control. We can only control ourselves as the outcomes partially depend on our response to the drawbacks we face in our lives.

Here, I will leave you with some points to ponder over that can help you understand why we should rule our moods and not let them rule us instead.

- My mother once told me, *"Cheer up; things could be worse."* I took her advice and cheered up. Sure enough, things did get worse. Keep smiling!

- It's nice to be important, but it's more important to be nice.

- *"It is difficult to find happiness within oneself, but it is impossible to find it anywhere else." -Arthur* **Schopenhauer**

- Joy does not come from happiness; happiness comes from joy!

- A forced smile is much better than a sincere frown!

- If you smile a lot, you will have as you get older a twinkle in your wrinkle!

- Don't let your EGO get in the way. EGO is Edging God   Out.

Chapter 7
Giving Generously

It is no secret that we all tend to become a little selfish in our lives from time to time. There are moments in our lives where we tell ourselves to forget about everything going on around us and to focus on ourselves. We are simply done with serving others, and so we delude ourselves into thinking that it is about time we serve ourselves.

There are many studies that even deem selfishness to be healthier in some aspects of life. However, it can become destructible if you allow it to cross certain limits in life. This feeling of serving yourself can completely destroy our lives without us realizing it.

We tend to overlook the destruction this emotion leaves in its wake until we reach the very end of our lives. There are many regrets we house in our hearts when we look back on our selfish acts in life. It is commonly believed that selfishness arises due to the lack of value for human life. Selfish people lack concerns, while at other times, they do not hold any value for those around them.

They are widely believed to treat others unfairly and unjustly. Selfish people tend to exploit others so that it is easier for them to put their pleasures before others. Selfishness makes a person act for themselves. They constantly seek out benefits for themselves and tell themselves, *"I am doing this for me because I need it."* However, selfishness is not as simple as that.

It is a broad topic that can mean anything related to a certain type of context. It is better to be selfish when you are trying to pursue your love interest, as it is widely accepted when you are being selfish to find happiness in life. We all want to live a healthy and happy life. It is natural to ensure that our food requirements are met before we can give it to those who are less privileged than us.

However, it is definitely not normal to put your own petty needs in front of the significant needs of those around you. Although many people agree that being selfish makes life easier. However, it can never fulfill a certain emptiness left in the hearts of selfish people. People tend to run away from those who are selfish. There are times when we cannot stand selfish people, and there comes the point in our lives where we simply get fed up with them before we decide to leave for good. Selfishness can be good as long as we do not hurt others in that process. If we look for ways to pursue our happiness that can bring harm to others, then there is no point in pursuing happiness in that manner. It is fine to be selfish as long as we do not hurt others with our selfish needs.

On the other side of the spectrum, we have the feeling of generosity, which is an exact opposite of selfishness. Generosity is one of the simplest emotions that we humans experience on a daily basis from time to time. Yet, we tend to make this more complicated than necessary when it comes to giving things with an open heart.

Sometimes we want to give more but end up serving ourselves more by ignoring the needs of others. Generosity and selfishness share an indirect relationship with each other. The more selfish you are, the less generous you tend to be because a person is too busy fulfilling their own desires by overlooking the desires of others around him.

The real problem lies in how warped up this world is becoming. It is easier for us to believe that being selfish can help us solve many problems in our lives. The world we live in today is vastly different from the world that used to exist before us. Today, it is harder for us to attain more things in life, as most of us are barely making an adequate living. Like I stated previously, the more you have, the less you want. The opposite is also true. The less you have, the more you want. There are so many things we want in our lives, but our reasons for wanting things differ from the things we actually need in life in order to lead it adequately. The need for materialism rises in us just because we want to show it off to those around us. We want to have a big house with white picket fences as well as a nice car just so that we can flex it around. Eventually, it becomes about us getting praised by those around us.

Running Towards Success

From a very young age, we are always told that we need to do better in our lives in order to be more successful. Our elders sell us the lie that we need to be successful in order to be happy in our lives. Being successful means being famous, rich, beautiful – someone who is admired by the masses. Therefore, we begin focusing on our lives on the notion of impressing others. We are conditioned by everyone to believe that our main goal in life must consist of acquiring success.

However, it is imperative to realize that success comes in different forms for many people. Success does not necessarily have to be elaborate. It can be as simple as living a standard life with everything you could ever need. Success, for some people, could be equal to acquiring a simple life with no debts hanging over their heads. The word 'success' does not have to stick to a single meaning in life. It can mean anything as long as you are living a life where you are happy and have everything you could ever need. Success does not have to be as materialistic as being rich. This line of thinking can actually lead us to materialism.

Materialism is all about acquiring possessions for the sole purpose of impressing others. One of the many traits all materialistic people share with each other is that they judge others by the number and quality of their possessions. They believe that possessions are vital to obtain happiness and openly judge others' success by sticking to their own version of success. Materialism does not necessarily have to be viewed as bad. The motives behind our need to acquire possession matter the most. So if you are the type of person who would buy a sports car just because you love driving fast cars, then you are not really a materialistic person, but rather you are just following your passion. On the other hand, if you buy a sports car just because you want to impress a group of people or a person for that matter, then you are a materialistic person by all means. Most people believe that buying things can lead them to happiness. We all go on a shopping spree sometimes just to cheer ourselves up without realizing that the happiness we obtain only lasts for a few minutes.

We realize that we want to buy more and more. Individuals who are materialistic are less satisfied and unhappy with their lives. They feel as if they are less competent as compared to others in their lives. Materialistic people also avoid social interactions with people because they feel incompetent as compared to others. This leads to creating weaker connections, and thus, it can hold the power to destroy relationships in general as they find human interaction less satisfying.

Everything boils down to why you buy a certain thing or do a certain thing in life. If you spend your life impressing others, then it means that you are spending your life in vain. It should not matter what others think of you.

What should matter the most is what you think of yourself.

Temporary Solution

One of our biggest misconceptions in this world is that we believe that happiness is a permanent solution to life. We all walk down the path to find happiness without realizing that it is an emotion that depends on external factors. Happiness should be one of the many goals in our lives, but it should not be the only goal left in our lives. People tend to go to great lengths just to be happy, and it gives rise to many factors such as selfishness and materialism. We all came into this world for a bigger reason than simply finding happiness.

We cannot simply believe in the delusions that happiness can stay with us forever. There are going to be ups and downs in our lives. There will be moments when we will be sad and beaten down. But even sadness can be viewed as a blessing because it helps us realize the value of happiness. We all need a little sadness in our lives to appreciate the happiness we experience in it. If we simply rely on the fact that there should only be happiness in our lives, then it means that we are wrapping ourselves in an illusion.

Happiness starts fleeting if we acquire it through materialism. The only thing we should keep in our minds is that our happiness truly depends on us. We can find happiness in every little thing if we look at this world from a positive perspective. Our happiness truly lies in how we react to the world around us. There are many people who have everything in their lives and still tend to feel an emptiness that can never be filled no matter what they do in life. They can go out and socialize all they want, but at the end of the day, they are still unhappy with their lives. They wallow in ungratefulness despite having more than what one could ask for. That is why happiness can never truly be achieved through materialistic things.

Permanent Solution

The easiest way to acquire long-term happiness is by practicing being generous in your daily life. Generosity is more than just an act of kindness. It can help in developing compassion for mankind. The willingness to give others the same things you would buy for yourself is a true act of selflessness. Practicing generosity can lead to living a happy and healthy life. There are a number of benefits that come along with being generous in your daily life. It helps in reducing stress, fights off depression, enhances a sense of purpose, and supports the physical health of individuals. People who are more generous in their lives are also admired and respected by many people around them. We always look up to those who surprise us by giving us what we want in our lives.

In a way, generosity can also be viewed as an act of selfishness as we act on it for our own personal interests. It also helps us feel better about ourselves whenever we gift others with the objects they want the most. Generosity can also boost our confidence as more people start behaving respectfully around us. Being generous also helps divert our attention from ourselves for a while.

It also creates awareness, and we become more sensitive toward what others need. Being generous can also help us with loving ourselves. Oftentimes, we tend to listen more closely to the inner voice in our heads that criticizes every single move of ours. By continuously listening to that inner voice in our heads, we start self-sabotaging ourselves by being more negative toward ourselves. We can mute that critical inner voice if we focus more on the world and people around us than on ourselves. It is healthy for us to focus on ourselves, our moves, and our actions, but we should also take a break to catch up on what others around us want in life.

Practicing Generosity

There are many ways one can practice generosity in their lives. You could simply buy an object you see that reminds you of your best friend, favorite colleague, or a really close relative. Being generous can be as easy as that. However, there are four common ways you can practice generosity in your life.

Being Sensitive to their needs

Generosity tends to be more effective when you offer gifts that are sensitive to others. It truly counts if you get someone something they really wanted or needed in their life. It does not necessarily have to be a materialistic thing.

You can go ahead and make something for them just to make them feel happy. Remember, it's the thought that counts and not the gift itself. Sometimes the greatest gift in the world you can give someone is your presence and attention when they are going through a tough phase in their lives. Being that person whom others can talk to is also an act of generosity because sometimes the only thing a person needs is someone to lean on and talk to about personal matters in order to feel better.

Accepting The Act

Most people have it easier when they are on the giving end. However, it is healthy to allow others to do things for you from time to time. Instead of feeling burdened when others do things for you, it is better to accept their act of kindness. As humans, we are prone to feel burdened when they gift us with things. We start getting the urge to return the act of kindness so that we do not feel as if we are freeloading on others.

This kind of feeling can also lead to depression and incompetence. The only way to tackle these negative feelings is that we start accepting others' generosity. This world may run on the give and take system, but we do not have to follow the same system when someone pulls on an act of kindness to make us feel happy. Accepting generosity may also feel uncomfortable for a while if you lived through a childhood where you were unloved and felt unworthy. But it is crucial to remember that generosity is an act of love, and it is important for us to act positively when it comes to being loved.

Accepting Appreciation

Appreciating others is one of the many ways to act when someone is being generous to you. It is crucial to remember that generosity can also help us get closer to others. Do not shy away from others when they openly appreciate you. Most of us tend to shrug whenever someone thanks us for something. At some points in our lives, we tend to respond with a, *"Oh, don't worry about it. It's nothing,"* whenever someone expresses their appreciation.

This can actually make the other person feel less competent and leaves them with a feeling of confusion. So next time someone thanks you for something, instead of replying with that conditioned response, always reply with an act of love or a big smile to show them that you are content with being appreciated.

Show Appreciation

Remember, generosity is not only about being appreciated but also appreciating those around you. It is imperative that you show others you appreciate them or their existence even if you are painfully shy in your life. Whenever someone gives us an exorbitant gift, we always respond with, *"This is too expensive!"* or *"You shouldn't have bought something so expensive."*

Sometimes we even go as far as rejecting the gift because it makes us feel too inferior to accept something expensive. As a result, this can negatively impact the giver and make them feel bad for making you feel uncomfortable. It is better to show them or tell them how much you truly appreciate them after **accepting** their gifts.

Generosity can also be viewed as an act of worship. There are many places within the Bible where they talk about generosity. If you are one of the lucky ones who have been blessed with everything they could need in life, then it is your duty to make sure you help those who are deprived of those basic necessities. Those who help others will always have everything in abundance. We should never hold ourselves back from helping others by thinking that we do not have enough for ourselves. We should always believe in God and know that He will always be the provider for us. A generous person will always prosper in life because they know what they have to do to attain long-term happiness. Helping others by guiding them toward their success will only help you in elevating your level of success.

Here are some points for you to ponder over the topic of generosity.

- *"Do your givin' while you're livin'… then you'll be knowin' where it's goin'." -**Ann Landers***
- We can't live forever, but our passions can!
- The joy of living is the joy of giving
- *"You make a living by what you get, but you make a life by what you give!" - **Sir Winston Churchill***
- You get more than you give when you give more than you get!

Chapter 8
Motives Matter

There are many moments in our lives that make us question our own existence. We label that moment as an 'existential crisis' and try to ease ourselves by the fact that every person goes through it. As humans, we are prone to labeling everything we come across in our lives so that it can help us create a better understanding of what we are going through.

Putting labels on everything is one of our favorite hobbies because it creates a sense of unification among different people. People in a group are only strangers to each other until they start discussing their problems with each other. There might be those who can easily connect with you because they are going through a similar experience in life. Sometimes we do not discuss our problems with others because we are seeking solutions.

Sometimes we merely have a discussion with someone else so that we can ease the burden in our hearts. Putting labels on everything becomes easier for us to convey what we are going through our lives. It not only gives us an idea of what it really is, whether it is an emotion or a disorder, but it also helps us relate with others. A number of people go through existential crises in their lives. At some point, we all question our purpose in this world. We all come across a certain point where we ask ourselves, *"What am I doing with my life?"* You could have the most stable job in the world, or run your own business, and have every comfort handed to you and still come across this question on a daily basis.

That is only because materialism can never fill the emptiness that aches in our chests from time to time. It is normal for humans to be unsatisfied with their lives. The reason is that we are all in search of our meaning and purpose in this world. The more we have, the more we want, and the more we start neglecting our needs.

As stated in the previous chapters, we surpass our needs just for our wants in this world. For example, a person might work day and night just to have enough money saved up so that they can buy the latest model of their current phone. They do not exactly need the latest model, but they try to work hard for it because they simply want it. During that process, the person overlooks their health and work extensively just to achieve that materialistic object in their lives. The object may bring them happiness for a while, but it will be temporary and will not last long as they would forget about it after a while. One of the most common examples to explain temporary happiness is by looking at our own behavior when we buy something new. We may cherish it and take care of it in the beginning, but we slowly get used to possessing it before we start tossing it around. The more carelessly we treat our objects, the more it points towards our temporary happiness.

This does not mean that you should undermine your hard work. Sometimes we all need to work hard in life to make achievements in our lives. Our biggest problem is that we depend more on our results than our motives behind the objective. We worry more about whether or not we will be able to reach the completion of our objective rather than focusing on our motives behind it.

But before we delve into the topic of motives, it is crucial for us to understand what it really is so that we do not confuse the term with 'intentions.'

What is the motive?

According to the oxford dictionary, 'motive' is defined as our reason to do something in our lives. On the other hand, intention provides us with the reason to do something in our lives. These two terms are entirely different from each other but are often confused as one due to the similarities between the words. However, these two words have totally different meanings in our lives. Our intentions point towards our aims, whereas motives provide us with a reason to achieve our goals in life.

Motives implicate the motivation we must possess in order to move forward in our lives. We also know that motivation is one of the many driving factors in our lives. A person without a motive is simply existing in their worlds and are not bothered to try living because they do not want to put that much effort in their lives. We all need some sort of motive to do or to achieve something in our lives.

However, we are all prone to being disheartened by certain factors that we come across in our lives. It is easy for us to lose our focus as we allow our emotions to control us. That is why, in the previous chapters, it has been stated that we should all control our emotions and not let them control us. Our emotions are reactions to the world, and we must understand that whatever goes on around us is out of our control. If someone dislikes us or says something to us, then we cannot control it. But we can control how we react to it. We tend to lose ourselves within the moment at times and do things that we later come to regret. It is important for us to understand that all of these things will be a part of our lives, no matter what. We have to learn from our mistakes so that we can build ourselves up from every point in life. The only motivation we need to create a better version of ourselves is by believing in the fact that we can turn our lives around for the better if we try.

But we cannot achieve greatness if we continuously keep asking ourselves for permission. We should stop questioning our own existence so that we can focus on our lives rather than on our mere existence. There are many reasons why a person exists in this world. Some people live for a number of reasons, such as leading a righteous life so that they can serve their Lord, or make their parents proud, and so on. We can never really run out of reasons when it comes to questioning our existence. However, there are some points in our lives where we lose our motivation or will to live. That is why we should stop questioning our own existence and work toward building motivation as it can help us achieve greatness in our lives. That greatness can provide you with long-term happiness if you work hard to achieve it for all the right reasons. One of the many reasons why you should stop questioning your existence is because questions give birth to doubts. Once you start doubting yourself is the moment you start doubting others too. You ask yourself whether the other person that you talk on a daily basis really likes you or is tolerating you because you are both existing in the same place at the same moment. You doubt the world that is showing you that it is real in many ways.

Doubts also give rise to carelessness, and we all make bad decisions in our lives once we truly stop caring about ourselves. The only way to make your life more exciting is by creating a goal for yourself. These goals will be the stepping stones that can help us achieve our dreams. But goals are only wishes if we do not act upon them. We all need some sort of motivation to achieve those goals. The only problem is that we are not born with motivation. It is a skill that is honed over a period of time. We all stall our motivation by telling ourselves some serious lies. We tell ourselves, *"I can do this some other time,"* Or *"I'll get to do that some other day,"* Or *"No, not today."* Or *"I'm too busy to focus on that."* If you are one of those people who would rather search for reasons to not do something in life, then it means that there is a severe lack of your beliefs. It is imperative to keep in mind that we have to build up our motivation ourselves. No one else can push us towards achieving anything in our life except for ourselves. We need to rely more on ourselves than on something as undetermined as 'time.'

You might spend the rest of your life waiting for the 'right time' and die without achieving anything you ever dreamt of. Or, you can simply take some time out of your hectic schedule and focus on yourself. One of the best parts of living in this world is that we are all provided with an abundance of choices. We can either choose to live a life where we are minimally satisfied, or we can choose to live a life where we make things happen ourselves. It is all about having a good thought that you can turn into immediate action. Motivation is one of the crucial factors that can help you in achieving anything you want in life. If there is no goal post for you, then you will not have any purpose to strive towards something in life. It is a life-skill that helps you by providing you with a purpose in life. In order to steward a purpose, it is important that you have the motivation that can help you work towards your goals. This, in turn, can help turn your dreams into reality and goals into a standard lifestyle. Keep in mind that you need to do this for your sake. Others can also provide you with motivation, so the company you keep around you can also impact you greatly. If you are surrounded by people who want to achieve greatness in life, then you will naturally be motivated to do the same.

We always pull ourselves into a loop of motivation by telling ourselves that if they can do it, then so can we. However, we need to come up with a solid foundation that can help us work towards our goal for the long term because we can also stop our own progress by not caring about what others did.

We live in a world where motivation has solved a number of problems in this world. It has produced many products that you use in your daily life. For example, if Bill Gates was not motivated to create Microsoft, then you would not be provided with an accessible application that is now used by everyone in this world. The only thing that can help you create greatness is the sense of self-confidence you possess in yourself. Having confidence can have a positive effect on relations and the world we all live in.

How to Motivate Yourself

There are many ways you can motivate yourself. A lot of factors can drive you toward motivation, but it is crucial to possess three important factors to be completely motivated.

Stay Positive

The only time we procrastinate in our lives is when we are in a bad mood. Our moods can greatly affect the amount of work we put in our lives. It may sound easier to remain positive, but it is one of the hardest things in the world. The only way you can remain positive is by reminding yourself about the motives you had in your mind when you first started out. Of course, you will be met with failure across the way, but every failure is just another step toward success.

It is, and it will always be a part of our lives. We can either be mad about it and stop our own progression, or we can tell ourselves that to live is to err. We will make mistakes, but those mistakes will not have the power to hold us back unless we allow it to. Everything in our life depends on us.

Reward Yourself

When you reach a certain milestone in life, it is crucial to reward yourself. Rewards can help you remain motivated and can help you work toward your goal. The way you reward yourself may be small or big, but it can help you in increasing your productivity. The more productive you are, the more positive you become, and the closer you get to your goals. Sometimes all you need to do in life is 'treat yourself' to remind yourself that you have gotten one step closer to your goal. This increases motivation almost magically.

Peer Pressure

According to science, peer pressure can help you more than actually hurt you. That is if you are being pressured to do better in some productive field in life. Peer pressure comes in all shapes, forms, and sizes. You have to pick the ones that can help you progress in the field of your interest. Surround yourself by those who strive hard to achieve success and watch yourself become one of them. It is important to keep in mind that you should always sit with those who share the same interests as you. If you surround yourself with a positive environment, only then will you be able to thrive on their energy. You can only achieve growth in both personal and professional fields of life if you motivate yourself to work harder. We are always going through one form of growth or another at every stage in life. Growth does not come with an age limit or time limit in life. Our mental growth will always be under process as long as we shall live. Your motivation will lead you toward making the right decisions in life.

Stepping outside the comfort zone is always a great way to grow in life. A lot of people question their existence when they either reach the lowest point in life or the point where they have achieved everything they could ever want.

It is up to us to make sure that we do not come across a dead-end in our lives. There is no such thing as just being a masterpiece.

No one ever said that you have to either be a masterpiece or a work in progress. You can be both simultaneously and still excel greatly in life. All you need to do is to make sure you motivate yourself enough to see another day in this world. Here I leave you with some points to ponder over that can help in providing you with your own motives. Remember, each person is unique, and we all adapt to our motives differently.

- Yesterday was a frustrating day! I put $5.00 in the change machine... and I'm still me.
- You cannot be it if you cannot see it.
- If you don't believe in yourself, then it is probably unanimous.
- A negative thought is a down payment on an obligation to fail.
- No one will be there to give you a push. You have to do it yourself!
- You can either simply exist with your current circumstances or resist them.

Chapter 9
Be Interested In Others

There are two types of people in this world; those who are curious and show interest in others and then those who are only concerned about themselves. It is a well-accepted fact that no one in this world likes a self-centered person. But this fact alone does not really stop people from being self-absorbed. There are many reasons why we hate people who are continuously self-centered and use the words 'me, I, my' occasionally on a daily basis. They make you feel left out even if you are simply conversing with them. They continuously use phrases that make you feel irritated. It is easier for people to cut off self-centered people because they feel a sense of relief when such people are out of your life.

Self-centered people also fill out one of the criteria present in the category list of toxic behaviors of an individual. Being around such people can damage your mental peace and make you feel inadequate for being yourself. Other than having people turn their backs, self-centered people are also prone to fall ill more quickly because of how much they stress about their own lives. It is healthy to worry about your life but not to the point where it starts affecting you physically. They stress so much about themselves where they reach a point that it neurologically starts affecting them. The word 'self-centeredness' has also been given different types of names throughout the years. The word 'self-centeredness' is also synonymous with self-obsessed, self-absorbed, self-preoccupied, and egotistical as well as selfish people around the globe. One of the biggest misunderstandings we have created is labeling self-centeredness as narcissism.

It is easy for us to throw the word 'narcissism' around loosely whenever we see someone who is merely conscious of what they are wearing or how they look on a daily basis. There are people who are labeled as narcissists simply because they post their own selfies on social media platforms. However, narcissists are more than just people who are obsessed with themselves.

The word may be used loosely, but the term 'narcissism' is anything but. According to Psychology, being a narcissist is an actual personality disorder. This is known as Narcissistic Personality Disorder. It is an actual mental illness that deludes a person into thinking that they are superior to everyone else in the world. Their traits have distinct differences from people who are self-absorbed. The fact that we confuse an actual personality disorder (narcissism) as a person's vanity says a lot about us as humans. It means that we are still unable to differentiate between those who actually need help with their mental illness with someone who can simply be guided to become a better version of themselves.

Despite living for hundreds of thousands of years, we are still unable to understand our own humanity. Our humanity is such a broad topic that even writing millions and trillions of books about it will never be able to uncover it. However, in this book, there will be just enough guidance for an average man to understand humanity. We can all start understanding tiny aspects about ourselves by learning how to differentiate between two closely related, but entirely different categories.

Difference between Narcissism and Self Centeredness

'Narcissist' is a term that is often used to describe a large variety of people in this world. We use this term to describe those whom we find to be difficult to get along with or downright offensive people. Due to the language of popular culture, this mental illness (like many others) is downplayed by the majority of people. Narcissistic Personality Disorder only affects 1% of the population and can only be labeled after undergoing a clinical trial. A slight spectrum of narcissism is also present in average humans. We all exhibit narcissism to some extent, but we remain on the healthy spectrum by reminding ourselves that we are just as human as others around us. People who care about themselves are not narcissistic but self-obsessed people. On the other hand, narcissistic people believe that they are special and exude assertiveness as well as confidence in huge waves.

They put themselves out there to accept any challenge that comes their way. Self-centered people share the same qualities but to an extent. A narcissistic person often feels entitled to have the best of everything. Their obsession with perfection goes on to the point where they would not think twice before sabotaging someone else just to secure their own position in both personal and professional life. This level of arrogance and grandiosity interferes with their daily functioning lives. In the end, they are unable to maintain long-lasting relationships in their lives.

With that being stated, not every self-centered individual is narcissistic, and as sensible creatures, we can clearly see why it can be bad for us. At the end of the day, a narcissistic person or a self-centered person will always be alone, and that loneliness can lead to a number of other mental illnesses in an individual. A lone person will always be surrounded by their negative thoughts, and that negativity will drive positive people further away from them.

The world we live in has so much to offer, and yet we spend most of our time thinking about ourselves. Sure, we all have to think for ourselves to live a proper life, but there are times when we completely stop focusing on others around us. We become too self-absorbed in our lives that we overlook those who need us the most. There are some people in this world who believe that it is somewhat 'cool' to not care about those who are around them. They do not show the slightest interest in those who are supposedly close to them and then label themselves as easygoing people who do not need friends to survive in this world.

They might be backed up with reasons, but any reason will not be good enough to go against human nature.

Social Animals

One of the greatest philosophers of all times once stated that humans are social animals by nature. Aristotle was the first philosopher who had uncovered one of the greatest mysteries behind why humans seek our other humans to make themselves feel more comfortable. His work shaped philosophy into what it is today. His tactics are used on a daily basis and well utilized in the field of psychology. According to Aristotle, humans cannot live without other humans.

We are social creatures who live to build connections around us. During the Stone Age Era, many cavemen sought out other cavewomen to create a family. Despite the lack of development in languages, they communicated with others to create tribes for better protection. They would build shelters together, and the females would take care of the children while the male went out to hunt for food. They heavily relied on each other to get their needs fulfilled. We may not be living in the cavemen era anymore, but our habits remain the same. We continuously seek others out to create connections with other people so that we can feel closer to them.

We rely on those around us to have our physical, emotional, and mental needs fulfilled by everyone around them. Today, we can still see that sociality is a dominant force that has shaped physiology, thoughts, languages, behavior, and neural activity.

We build societies to create a sense of belonging and to help those who need it the most during their time of need. From creating tribes to societies, we excelled at creating a platform where people can work together for the betterment of our world. Society is a system created by people belonging to different races, religions, ethnicities, and identifications.

They come together to form a platform that welcomes anyone who shares the same set of opinions with them. Societies have helped humans create connections around the world. It is the easiest way to create harmony and a loving environment. People living in a society are not related to each other in any shape or form. They share the connection of trust, understanding, and comfort to elevate a person. There are many societies that use their authority negatively, but it is crucial to remember that we are also members of society. Even a single person in society can bring a drastic change by convincing others to follow the right path. .Even if a person has convinced themselves that they do not need to rely on anyone else but their own selves, then they do not mean that they do not crave human connection from time to time. It is in our human nature to seek someone, anyone, during the toughest parts of our lives. The best part is that we get to be there for those who are desperately reaching out to us.

These connections we build may not all produce positive results, but we should all keep in mind that good and bad experiences come in every stage of our lives. Every good experience makes us seek out more, but we suddenly stop when we come across a single bad experience. Why do we self-sabotage ourselves in this manner?

It is important to remember that there will always be someone out there who will provide you with a better experience even after you go through a bad one. We need to create connections in order to survive and thrive in life.

As stated in previous chapters, our environment and the company we choose to live with affect us greatly. If we choose to surround ourselves with positive people, we start exhibiting positivity ourselves.

This alone explains why we need to start showing an interest in others and get out of our own personal bubble. Do not stop yourself from showing interest in others. There are many people who view showing an interest as 'lame' and 'uncool,' but the truth is that nothing can be more plentiful than being curious about others. This curiosity is often deemed as bad, but then again, we also confuse curiosity with invasiveness. These two terms are different.

Curiosity leads to questions, whereas invasiveness leads to enforcing your solutions on other's problems. One must always remember to allow others to open up when they are comfortable with being themselves. Interest can lead us to opportunities that can help us invest in other's life. We do not have to give someone money to show them we are invested in them.

A kind gesture is more than enough to show them how much you truly value them and their companionship. Remember, materialistic things only give them temporary happiness. Whenever someone reminisces about a person, they do not talk about how many things that person gave them, but they reminisce about how that person was there for them when they needed it the most.

They do not say, *"Oh, she gave me a Gucci bag as a present,"* but state, *"That person was really kind to me, and she didn't even know that she boosted up my confidence on a daily basis."* These acts of kindness can never be labeled as little. Giving more to others when your plate is full can lead to soulful happiness.

One of the many ways to serve God is by serving His creation. Some of us might feel like being served all the time by people around them. But it is our duty, as decent human beings, to serve others whenever we are capable of doing so. Doing something for others, no matter how small or unplanned it is, can boost our own happiness powerfully when we see how much they appreciate it.

Even if they do not appreciate it (remember, you cannot control other's actions), you can still tell yourself that you tried your best and move on. Serving others can bring happiness, and that can lead to life satisfaction as it provides us with a sense of purpose. It also boosts our sense of competency and improves our moods. Once our moods are improved, it can easily reduce stress in our lives. Kindness is the conduit that can guide us toward happiness. A person who goes through the worst betrayal either turns out to be a bitter person or into someone who is often viewed as too kind for this world. The choice lies in our own hands. The best way to connect with others is to make sure you exude genuine kindness. Do not just do it for the sake of your own self but truly for the sake of others. Serving others can lead to a successful life as it helps in creating better connections in the world.

Here, I leave you with some points that can help you understand why being interested in others is a good choice.

- To be successful, you must serve, not be served
- Shout praise and whisper criticism
- He who receives a good turn should never forget it; he who does one should never remember it.

Chapter 10
Live One Day at a Time

Our past, present, and future are just more than adjectives in dictionary books. Our entire life is explained in these three words, which also happen to be the phases of our lives. Most people believe that only the lucky ones are able to experience these three different phases in their lives. But the truth is that luck has nothing to do with how you lead your life. It is a figment of people's imagination that was created to make them feel better about their own lack of progression in life. A person's life cannot be defined by something, such as luck.

The concept of luck is simply as evasive as our desperation to overlook our own problems in life. These three phases may be different but are always merged with each other due to a lack of better understanding. There are times when people carry their past forward into their future by thinking about the present. Our first phase of life may be crucial for shaping our mindset and personality, but there is always a possibility for improvement as we move forward in our lives.

The real thing that troubles us the most is that some of us still have not let go of our pasts. We are still shackled by the mistakes and failures we experienced in our lives. A lot of people tell us to move on from the past, but we also know that it is easier said than done. The past is a crucial part of our life as it teaches us lessons in a hard way. At some point in our lives, we reach our lowest and are unable to look past that point even though the bad time has passed.

We make the mistake of allowing it to become a part of us, and that is when the real issues emerge in our daily lives. Every moment we live in today will become a part of our past at some point in life. There is no way we can simply move on when we experience something painful in our lives. Nothing ever remains the same after a particular ground-breaking moment we experience from time to time.

The biggest problem is that we always brace ourselves for the worst before it can even occur. We feed ourselves with lies because we do not want to be hurt by others. We give our past too much power than we would like to admit. No matter how far you go in life, if you hold onto the past, then you are not truly living in the present. The past now has power over you, and you mold yourself according to the experiences you go through. Of course, we are all shaped by experiences, both good and bad, but it is always important to remember who we really are. Sometimes we allow others' opinions about ourselves affect us to the point where we actually become what they think about us. We let go of our reality and allow theirs to merge with ours because we constantly think about it. The more we think about it, the more we allow it to affect us greatly. It is important to keep in mind that no one can have an impact on you unless you allow them to. We are too wrapped up in our lives that we often forget that we have power over ourselves and not the other way around. No one is your boss except for yourself.

It is imperative to integrate things that will help us progress in our lives, but that is a long procedure. Every person heals at their own pace as they move along with time, and there is no such thing as 'moving on.' But yes, there is such a thing as 'living in the present.' Our past may weigh on us because of the struggles we go through. We have all seen bad days at some point in our lives, but we have also allowed our past struggles to interfere with our present lives. We all carry the fears we have experienced in our pasts into our presents.

It also shapes our future as more fear only holds us back from ever moving forward in time. The only way to know if you are allowing your past to affect you is by wondering about your present. Do you still feel like you have not made progress in life? Do you still feel stuck in the same place you were at five years ago? Are you still thinking about times such as 'back then' in your current time? Then maybe it is time for you to reevaluate your life and understand that the only reason why you are stuck in the past is that you are still living in it.

The past does not dissolve with time, but it dissolves with your mindset. The only reason why you are unable to move forward is that you are unable to let go of yesterday. It is entirely impossible for you to move forward into your future if you are unable to let go of your past. Another adversary you face while holding onto your past is that you suddenly stop focusing on your present.

Let the Past Rest

Carrying your past forward in life can be burdensome at times. Our struggles will always weigh heavily on our shoulders, and this weight can hold us back from living in the moment. It also stops us from reaching our highest potential in life. The only way we create our own problems is by providing those problems with an identity of their own. Everything you do is given an identity of its own. You call yourself 'financially unstable' when you are unable to pay for your own basic necessities in life. You call yourself 'mentally drained' when you have a tiring day.

You call yourself 'too busy' just to avoid interactions with other people. There are so many things we have identified as a part of our lives that we have forgotten who we truly are. There are people who are still unable to let go of the struggles they faced in the past just to reach the highest peak in their lives. This only prevents them from being truly satisfied with their lives, and as a result, they find themselves living in the past.

The real question is if we are afraid to let go of our past because we have become too attached to our struggles and failures in life? Are we unable to move forward because we do not know how to adjust to our present without experiencing hardships in life? There are also people who have a wonderful past and come across a terrifying present where they lose everything in their lives.

There are many stories of people going from zero to hero, and vice versa. Then there are those who had everything and suddenly find themselves back at square one. The first phase they enter is denial, which is followed by anger and depression before acceptance finally begins. They pick themselves up so that they can go back to living a life full of luxuries. Many people use their past as a driving factor to unlock a better future for themselves, but holding onto the past for a longer period of time can prevent you from living in the present.

Letting go of the past is nowhere near easy. It is harder to let go of negative experiences, false beliefs, unhealthy relationships, and bad habits. We allow the ruminations to shape our actions and our present by holding onto things that are better left off. Holding onto the past can prevent you from seeing the beauty of the present moment as well as it prevents you from entering the healing phase in life. You cannot experience true happiness and joy unless you forgive yourself and others who harmed you in the past. Let the past rest before you become a part of it.

There are three crucial reasons why you should let go of the past:

The Past Cannot Be Changed

We always tell ourselves, *"Why did I say that?"* *"Why did I do that?"* *"I should have done better!"* *"I wish I never met that person.",* or *"I wish I could erase my mistakes."* And so we trap ourselves in a loop of monologue where we berate ourselves on a daily basis. The only reason why we do this to ourselves is that we are unable to accept the fact that the past cannot be changed. We all wish for a time machine so that we can go back and correct all our wrongs. We all seek for second chances without realizing that we will always be provided with new chances as long as we live. The past cannot be changed, but the good news is that we can always learn from the mistakes we make on a daily basis.

Open Your Mind

The mind is a sacred space for every person in this world. The only limitations we impose on ourselves are all in our heads. Literally, it is all in our heads and nothing more. We only stop ourselves when we provide those limitations with an identity. Letting go of the past can allow you to remove the mind-blocks present in your head and create a space for something new to grow. The setbacks you faced in the past may have been a crucial part of your life, but they do not have to define you as a person. The moment you let go of the hardships is the moment you will be able to feel excited about living. This world is full of opportunities that are waiting to be discovered by you, and the only way you can experience them is by stepping out of the past and focusing on your future.

Liberation

True liberation comes with a mind that is open to experience new and exciting things in life. This can provide you with a sense of liberation and freedom that you have never experienced before. Liberation is more than just gaining a new sense of freedom. Your choices become clear to you the moment you liberate yourself and break yourself free from the shackles of your past.

Imagine that you are carrying your past physically with you. There is a backpack full of stones, and each stone represents the mistakes, setbacks, adversaries, and painful experiences you have endured in the past. How much longer do you think you will be able to walk with that heavy bag until you finally get tired of moving forward? You will simply tell yourself that you are taking a rest and then find yourself stuck for the rest of your life. There are two choices you can make at that moment. You can either leave the bag full of burdens behind or decide to take it with you. More mistakes will be added in that bag until you finally decide to give up. The physical representation can help you understand why it is deemed foolish to allow the past to be heavy on your mind. There is only so much you can store in that head of yours until it finally explodes.

It is about time we allow the past to rest so that we can move forward in life. The other choice of leaving the bag behind in order to walk ahead can help you understand why it is important to leave the past where it belongs. We should make amends with our past, and then we should accept and heal before we can take another step forward in life. That is the moment when you will feel truly liberated in your life.

The best way to let go of our past is to go through a healing process. It is better to accept the fact that there is no way we can change our past or go back in time again. The only burdens we carry mentally affect us greatly until we decide to give up on ourselves.

Living in the present allows us to focus on our surroundings. We can truly appreciate our presence if the past is not holding us back. Either we allow the past to hold us back, or we allow the fear of the future to mess up our lives. We try so hard to focus on our past and future that we forget to simply live in the moment. That does not mean you do not focus on your future planning.

It simply means you give your present as much importance as you give to your future. The future is undecided, the past is confirmed, and the present is meant to be discovered. Would you really focus on something that has not been decided yet, or focus on something that cannot be changed no matter what you do? Or would you finally allow yourself to grow in life by focusing on the adventure known as the present? The choice lies in your mind, and you are free to opt for anything you can do.

It is about time we realize that these three different phases of our past, present, and future are not meant to be merged. We live to experience these phases at different points in our lives. The past you think of today was once your present, so if you want to change anything about it, then you can opt to make sure you never repeat the same mistake twice in your current present. We do not belong in the past, nor do we belong in the future we have for ourselves in our heads. We belong here, in this moment, where we can truly see our lives with the utmost clarity. What more do we need in life other than some clarity? The only way we can live with clarity is by living one day at a time.

Here I leave you with some quotes that can help you understand why living in the present is important.

- Live for today, dream for tomorrow, learn from yesterday.
- Today is the tomorrow you are worried about yesterday.
- Our grand business in life is not to see what lies dimly in the distance, but to do what lies clearly at hand.

Chapter 11
Hobbies

We all come across a stage in our lives where we tell ourselves that we need a break. The world we live in today is running at a fast pace, and we are always doing our best to catch up to it. We chase after things without thinking twice about needing it in our life. We all live our lives mapped out by the basic rules. Grow up, graduate, get a good job, buy a moderate-sized house, settle down with a spouse, create a family, and live happily ever after.

This is drilled into our heads from a very young age, and we do our best to focus on these goals without realizing what we actually want in life. We all do things differently, but we have created this basic map of achieving everything which others have done in their lives. Our goals drive us to the point where we reach the peak of our being burnt out. We experience a burn out from our adult life due to the fact that we barely pay any attention to ourselves when we are too busy working hard for our goals.

We chase too much in hopes of getting everything that we overlook our own needs from time to time. We spend our entire life trying to kill that inner child who is still telling us to do something reckless and fun from time to time. There are people who stop themselves from sitting on the swings because they believe that they are 'too old' for that. And then there are those who stop themselves from playing with the sand and creating sandcastles whenever they go to the beach because they do not want to look odd in the eyes of strangers.

The truth is that we have accepted the lies the world told us when they forced us to grow up. The inner child is slowly killed over the years as we focus on checking off our wish-list. Everything comes with a price, and we pay it at the cost of our inner child, who simply wants to have a day of rest and fun.

This world is progressing at a faster pace, and we have to work harder to ensure that we stay in the same loop as others. We do not want to feel left out, and hence, we start molding ourselves according to the desires we feel. We fail to realize that the tasks we do outside our work often contribute toward our success as it relieves us to take our minds off some of the stress we face in our daily lives. While stress may be good for you, it can truly be harmful if it exceeds the safe limit. There is a difference between positive and negative stress, which we come across from time to time. One of the best ways to handle stress is by distracting yourself from your daily life and doing something that actually relaxes you. That is why it is healthier to integrate certain hobbies into your daily lives. Hobbies can also help us in creating a better social circle as well as they can help in honing our skills. Having hobbies builds up our confidence and helps us focus on cultivating other skills.

A hobby does not necessarily need to be unrelated to our work. We actually turn our hobbies into our profession if we work really hard for them. Hobbies help us in honing our skills that can create more opportunities for us. However, the main factor we need to focus on while selecting our hobbies is to avoid taking on too much stress in life. Consider the level of stress you are put through on a daily basis and choose your hobby. Some people might choose games that might cause them more stress than relief in life, and our main purpose should be picking out the hobbies that do not add more stress to our lives. Secondly, it is imperative to choose the hobbies that would be more challenging so that we can actually enjoy doing them. The hobbies do not necessarily need to have a learning curve but can be somewhat related to education as well. Focusing on education hobbies can refine our thinking skills to a whole another level. Thirdly, we should always choose a hobby that can help us focus on something we are good at. A person should always pick out what they like to do in their free time rather than going on other's whims and suggestions.

Why We Should Have Hobbies
Creativity Skills

Most of the hobbies that are practiced around the world require creativity and skills. The creativity skills we develop during the process of having hobbies can directly help us implement them at our work. Through the process of creating creativity skills, we open our minds to many possibilities that can be implemented in different ways. For example, you will start having more ideas about how to reach the optimum results by implementing different creative methods in your job. What we do for fun can also help us progress in our profession by lowering our stress levels.

Reduce Stress

As stated, stress should be one of the driving factors that can help you develop a hobby of your own. Hobbies can provide us with a gateway to distract ourselves from our daily tasks. They can provide us with the break we need from time to time while reducing our level of stress simultaneously. There are times when hobbies require different levels of physical activities to create some chemical changes in our body that can contribute to reducing stress.

For example, a person who works at a desk job would most probably opt for a hobby that would require more physical work, and a person who works a laborious job would go for a hobby that requires minimal physical activity. It is important to keep in mind that we should always choose those types of hobbies that align with the needs of our bodies.

Boost Confidence

There are many hobbies that boost our confidence if we choose to do something we are good at. Learning something new on a daily basis makes us feel good about ourselves, and it only makes us yearn to learn new things. This can greatly impact our professional life because we will always be eager to try out new things at work as well.

Personal Development

Creativity and confidence may contribute to personal development, but it does not end there. We can transform our hobbies into many skills if we work hard for them, and that, in return, adds to our personal progress in life. The skills we develop while carrying out our hobbies can end up contributing to our professional field as well.

Structure Time

The hardest part of choosing a hobby is getting past the beginner's stage. It can even prove to be stressful if you are someone who is easily frustrated by a few drawbacks. However, the end results can prove to be worth it if you keep working on it till the very end.

One of the greatest reasons why implementing hobbies is crucial for our personal and professional growth is because they promote flow in our lives. You also appear interesting in other people's eyes as you will always have something great to talk about with people around you. This adds more layers to your identity as well as richness to the conception you have of yourself. We all want to surround ourselves with people who perform productively, but it is also important to be productive ourselves so that we can attract more people to do the same. The moment people look up to us is the moment we have achieved our highest potential, and that means we can only go higher from that point onwards.

The benefits you reap during the time you are developing your hobby will inspire you to do something else other than focusing on your profession. In this way, you can also easily avoid getting burnt out at work. It not only takes your mind off your work, but it also makes you feel like you are doing something productive for your own sake.

To find the perfect hobby, it is crucial to keep two points in your mind. In order to select a perfect hobby, always make sure that you do something that can help you with the following three aspects:

Make Money

The world runs on money, and although it should not be the only focus. However, it should be present in our list of priorities. Making money will make you feel more productive and only urge you to push harder to do something more. The money that is earned from something you love holds a different place in our hearts. When your habits help you in making money, then it is labeled as a hobby.

Keep in Shape

It is important to keep our physical and mental health in shape. Hobbies elevate our critical thinking skills by increasing our brainpower. We all need a change of scenery and maintaining hobbies that require physical movement can help us tremendously.

Life has a strange way of bringing us down, but hobbies are the only things that can pull us back up in life. Hobbies can drive you with passion for life while planting hope for tomorrow. To make life more enjoyable, find the hobbies that you can truly love.

Here, I leave you with a point to ponder over that can help you in finding the right hobby for yourself.

It is not about doing what you like but about liking what you do. That is the true secret of happiness.

Chapter 12
Always Keep Close to God

Problems are an integral part of our lives. They will always arise, no matter how much we try to prevent them. We can take as many precautionary steps as we would like, but it would still not prevent the things that are bound to occur. Taking too much caution can also prove to be bad for health if people practice it in their day-to-day tasks.

A cautious person only grows up to be more paranoid as they take each step forward in life with thoughts that hold them back. Caution is a healthy trait, but too much of anything can prove to be fatal for our health. This trait can prove toxic if it is implemented in daily tasks to the point where an individual questions themselves five times before doing something in their lives.

The cautious behavior is developed after a person goes through one problem or another. The thing about living in this world is that we will always be faced with troubles no matter how financially stable we really are or how much we surround ourselves with a loving family. These problems prevail because we have distanced ourselves from the real purpose of this life. Our real purpose does not lie in achieving a bigger house, the fastest car, the most beautiful family, and more money than we can count. In fact, our real purpose lies in being close to God, who has bestowed everything great down upon us. There are many beliefs that circulate around the topic of religion today that make us avert from it. The media is always talking about some terrorist killing people because of their religion, or people being killed because of the faith they follow.

The topic of religion may be full of controversies, but it does not truly reflect the religion itself. There have been instances when mankind has refused to acknowledge the presence of a greater power just because they are unable to completely understand it. We are all afraid of things we do not understand at all. This fear only holds us back more so that we are unable to divulge into the topic and see for ourselves what religion truly is. For some people, it may be a tale filled with conspiracies and gathers a large number of followers who are seeking redemption for their mistakes. For others, it is nothing but a hoax that was emerged to create a sense of belonging for people.

But religion is more than just what the majority perceives it to be. Remember, the way we view the world only reflects back on who we really are. You do not have to follow the basic definition of a particular religion just to feel closer to God. The fact is that God is always here with us in every moment of our lives. God is not found during the meditation period, either. Some people only meditate to talk to their Gods. There are many religions in this world, but their aim remains the same.

They believe in a higher power because they know that everything in this world did not simply come into existence on its own. There is a life that prevailed on this earth and carried messages to mankind. These messages always focused on creating a better version of yourself and following the rules to lead a lawful life. The concept of good and bad did not emerge out of nowhere. It is religion that helped others in identifying between the good and the bad. Religion informed people of their basic human rights and gave people a way to create a better environment for themselves. Today, we have drifted away from God because we simply cannot bring ourselves to focus on that aspect of our life anymore.

We are too busy to even take some time out of our hectic schedule to focus on ourselves, let alone try to focus on everything around us. One of the greatest news is that God will always be waiting for you even if you have abandoned Him. He will always be there for you during the darkest period of your life, just like He was there when you were blessed. You may not be able to see Him because you have lost your connection, but He will always watch over you.

God can be seen in everything we do in our daily lives. He is there even when you fall. It is His way of showing you that you can be stronger in this world. He will do His best to humble you down whenever you get too far ahead of yourself in your life. You see, God is not just some higher power who is hiding in the clouds.

He has not forgotten about you. He is more than just an entity as He has created you. Every minute you live through has been planned by Him. How wonderful it is to know that He has everything planned out for you, and He will only show you enough light so that you can guide yourself towards your destiny. His plans will always have something better in store for you. He will never put you through anything that tough when He knows you will be able to overcome it. He puts us all through hardships just to test our capabilities from time to time. It is His way of reminding you that He is ever-prevalent and waiting for you to come back to Him. This world is a beautiful place, and there might be some bad people who make the entire experience horrible, but it is important to remind ourselves that we do not have to become one of those dreadful people. Although some hardships may seem impossible for you to overcome, it is important to keep in mind that these hard times have been handed to you because God believes that you can overcome them.

These hardships are created to test whether we will go back to God and seek His comfort or not. These tests can help us focus more on ourselves than we actually realize. Such tests bring us to a temporary pause and make us question everything around us. The best way to tackle an existential crisis is to remember that God has brought you to a certain situation or made you born into a certain situation because He has plans for you. The best we can do in this world is to become a better version of ourselves as we tackle one hardship after another. These tests will help you understand your world around you.

The best part is that He never puts you through hardships alone. He is always there with you, around you, near you, and choose to come to you in different forms. Every solution you come up with to tackle the problem is His light shining on you. Whenever a person who goes through severe depression or experience momentary sadness, they often dwell and berate themselves for it. Talking to God when you are at your lowest is one of the many healthiest solutions to this problem. In order to get close to him, one must follow the rules of life that need to be implemented in order to get on God's favorite side.

A lot of people ask for evidence when they ask about God. *"You can't see him, so He's not real!"* People say this whenever they see someone meditating or doing whatever they can to calm themselves down. But these people should also know that God is not an invisible entity.

He is there in every shade of flower you see. He is present in the wind that whips against our faces, the coldness we feel, the snow that falls, the rain that thunders down, the elaborate design of plants, the soil that gives birth to different species of plants, the sea that houses a number of different creatures down to an ant are all indicators of God's presence.

He comes in different shapes and sizes. Sometimes He wears the form of our saviors and shows up in the form of solutions. You do not have to see God to know that He is real. You have to feel His presence just to know that He is near us.

There are many reasons why you should try to get near to God. However, there are three crucial reasons that can help you understand its importance.

Serenity

You can only achieve a true sense of peace after you get close to God. Being near God can help you experience peace. The sense of serenity only arises when we know that there is a higher power out there who is looking out for you. He creates a sense of reliability that helps you realize that you are not alone in this world. *"Come to me, all you who are weary and burdened, and I will give you rest. Take my yoke upon you and learn from me, for I gentle and humble in heart, and you will find rest for your souls. For* *my yoke is easy, and my burden is light." -**Matthew 28:11-30***

Have you ever seen a person who always looks happy despite the problems they go through in their daily lives? You might have wondered, *"Why doesn't this fellow look troubled even though he has one problem after another piling up on him?"* Well, the answer may be simple. The person simply believes that some higher power is looking after them. They know that God is always there with them, and they entrust Him with all of their sufferings. A new form of peace is achieved when you get closer to God and rely on Him every time something goes wrong.

Strength

God only pushes the problem onto us to test our strength, and He will never burden us with troubles that we cannot handle in our lives. God will pull the load off us whenever we walk closely with God. We are dependent on God whenever we are close to Him, and that provides us with the strength we need to continue with our daily tasks. Sometimes our problems may seem bigger to us, due to which we spend our entire time worrying about what to do next. These world-shattering problems may be big, but nothing can be bigger than God's plans. Everything He does is for our own good. We may not be able to see why it is good for us whenever we go through adversaries in life, but in the near future, we will always be thankful for the lessons taught to us by God's grace.

*"The Lord is the strength of his people, a fortress of salvation for the anointed one." -**King David***

When you are closer to God, He bestows you with divine strength that you can exhibit in your daily life. We all need strength to move on with this life. As humans, we believe that nothing can be worse than death. However, dying is easy, whereas living is difficult. You need strength to survive in this world.

Without strength, we cannot even survive in this world, let alone live our lives to the fullest. It takes an immense amount of strength to laugh and smile even when you feel like you are breaking from the inside. The only thing that is holding you together from breaking down is the leap of faith you take when you believe God is listening to your cries even if it's silent.

Guidance

"Whether you turn to the right or to the left, your ears will hear a voice behind you saying, 'This is the way; walk in it." **-Isaiah 30:21**

Faith gives birth to compassion for mankind. When you hold compassion in your heart for others, you eventually start developing compassion for yourself. One of the biggest mistakes we make is that we berate ourselves for every mistake we make in our lives. These mistakes often hold us back from progressing in life and keep us chained to our past in one way or another.

We blame ourselves without realizing that it was God who led us toward that mistake to teach us a lesson. He has a great plan for us, but we can only walk on that path of goodness by listening to His voice. He speaks to us in different ways. A common man may not hear His voice, but His message always comes across to us in different forms and shapes. His voice may be that little tick in your mind that is guiding you towards a particular purpose, a thing, or a person in your life. God also sends His messages to us through other people.

We often call such people as our 'guardian angels,' and they probably were sent by God with a purpose of their own. Communicating with God is important and can help us get closer to him in more ways than just one. He is the one who provides us with eternal peace, guides us, and provides us with directions in life. He gives us strength because He knows that it is impossible for mankind to go without it. God will always be there for us, even when we least expect it.

No matter what sin we commit in this world, He will never turn His back on you because He is ever forgiving. He will always be there for us, even when we believe that we have been abandoned by Him. God will never abandon us for we are His creations, and every flaw we see is just another trait given to us by Him.

These flaws can never truly be our flaws, for He creates nothing but perfection. He has given us enough freedom to make our own choices, and the flaw only lies in the decisions we make from time to time. The answer to our problems does not lie in this world, but rather it lies with God. We need to hear His voice, listen to His guidance, and do our best to not suppress the message of God.

"To shine on those living in darkness and in the shadow of death, to guide our feet into the path of peace." **-Luke 1:79**

God will always guide those, even if they are shrouded in the darkness of sins and despair. He will turn this darkness and despair into a light that will shine upon them when they atone for their sins with a clean heart and clear mind. He will light their path with guidance and provide them with peace of heart and mind. God will always reward mankind once they turn to him for help.

*"In their hearts, humans plan their course, but the LORD establishes their steps." -**Proverbs 16:9***

We all map out our plans in this world. We all have certain desires and goals in our hearts that we want to accomplish in our lives, no matter what. We all aspire to be greater beings in our lives. We want to be doctors, lawyers, businessmen and businesswomen, chemical and mechanical engineers, and so on. We want to obtain a prestigious post in our professions without realizing that we should always aim to be a better person in this world. We all want to become a great 'somebody' that we forget to become a great 'someone'.

Our plans may not always be carried to completion, but we should always remind ourselves that the plan we have for ourselves will never be as grand as God's plan.

Always stay close to God, for He will only guide you and provide you with eternal peace in this world.

*"The LORD makes firm the steps of the one who delights in him; though he may stumble, he will not fall, for the LORD upholds him with his hand." -**Psalm 37:23-24**

Here, I leave you with some points to ponder over that can help you understand the importance of being close to God.

- God would not have put a dream in your heart if He had not already equipped you with what you need to accomplish that dream.
- God is like a SCOTCH TAPE. You can't see Him, but you know He's there.

- God is like the U.S. POST OFFICE. Neither rain, nor snow, nor sleet, and nor ice will keep Him from His appointed destination.

Chapter 13
And Then It Is Winter

You know, time is the strangest thing in our lives. It has a way of moving quickly and catching up with you in a spur of a moment. You spend all your time completely unaware of the years that pass us by. It feels like just yesterday I was a young man, just married and embarking on my new life with my mate. Yet, in a way, now it seems like eons ago, and I simply cannot bring myself to wrap my head around it. Time feels like a car passing by.

You never really notice it until or unless it crashes into you. That is what time feels like to me, and it has me reeling back with the impact it leaves on me. I wonder where all the years went. I wonder when my moments turned into memories. Everything took place right before my eyes, and somehow, it still does not feel real to me. I know that I lived all of these years, but I never truly realized it or felt it as much as I did right now. I have glimpses of how it was back then and of all my hopes and dreams. I know that these moments I lived in my life have become a part of my memories.

As hazy as they are, they are still stored back in my mind, but now I know that it will all be forgotten one by one as I live past the age of eighty-eight. I always felt like I had enough time to think about it. But, here it is, the winter of my life and it catches me by surprise. It makes me wonder, *"How did I get here so fast? Where did the years go, and where did my youth go?"* It feels surreal. I remember the time I used to watch older people throughout the years and wonder what they were going through now. I used to think that those older people were years away from me and that winter was so far off that I could not fathom it or imagine fully what it would be like.

But, here it is. My friends are retired and getting grey. They move slower now, and I see an older person in them. Some are in better shape, and some are in worse shape than I am in, but I see the great change. Not like the ones that I remember who were young and vibrant. But I see them like me; their age is beginning to show, and we are now those older folks that we used to see and never thought we'd be. Each day now, I find that just getting a shower is a real target for the day! And taking a nap is not a treat anymore.

It's mandatory! Because if I don't do it out of my own free will, then I just fall asleep where I sit! And that is how I entered into this new season of my life. I was completely unprepared for all the aches & pains, and the loss of strength and ability to go and do things that I wish I had done but never did! At least I know that though the winter has come, and I'm not sure how long it will last, but I know that when it's over on earth... it's over. But there will not be an ending. It will just be the beginning of a new adventure.

Of course, like any other person, I have some regrets that I will be taking with me. There are some things that I wish I had not done and things that I should have done. It will always be in the back of my mind because of how much time I have to think about it. Indeed, there are many things I did in my life that I am happy with. It's all in a lifetime. If you are someone who is not in your winter yet, then let me remind you that it will be here faster than you think. So, whatever you would like to accomplish in your life, please do it quickly! Don't put things off for too long! Because it will be too late before you even realize it. Life goes by quickly that you do not even have time to think about what you did two weeks ago.

Do what you can do today as you can never be sure whether this is your winter or not! There is no guarantee that you will see all the seasons in your life. Your winter might arrive without autumn, so do your best to live for today and say all the things that need to be said. Say things that your loved ones want to remember. Hopefully, they will appreciate and love you for all the things that you have done for them in all of the years that have passed.

Planted in the house of the LORD, they will flourish in the courts of our God. They will still bear fruit in old age; they will stay fresh and green, proclaiming, *"The LORD is upright; he is my Rock, and there is no wickedness in him."* *-Psalm 92:13-15*

A lot of us ask ourselves if we have any purpose in our lives. We go through existential crises and try to find what we really want in this world. We try to search for different meanings without realizing that we will always have a purpose in this world as long as we have a pulse. Our purpose will stay with us as long as we have a heartbeat and thoughts in our heads.

"Your eyes saw me unformed, yet in Your book, all my days were written before any of them came into being."

-Psalm 139:16

God gave us a purpose in this world. He wrote down all of our days before they even happened. If you truly believe that your life is in your control, then you are gravely mistaken. Everything that happens in your life is planned and has a purpose. No matter where we are in life, we must never give up on our sense of purpose.

"Life" is a gift to you. The way you live your life is your gift to those who come after you. Be sure to make it a fantastic one. A lot of us are always in a hurry to get a lot of things done in life. We tend to think, *"Oh, I am rushing, rushing till life is no fun. All I get to do is live and die. But I am still in a hurry, and I don't know why!"* Well, it is because you sometimes feel like you are running out of time. But that is just the world running tricks on you.

You will never be too late or too early when it comes to making achievements in your life. No, you will always be right on time because we are not competing with others' time-scale. It is not necessary to have a good job by the age of twenty-five or be settled down before you hit your thirties. There will only one time to do those things, and that is the 'right time.' Life will never come back around for you again, so live it well. ENJOY TODAY! DO SOMETHING FUN! BE HAPPY! HAVE A GREAT DAY!

Remember that it is health that is the real wealth and not pieces of gold and silver.

LIVE HAPPY IN 2019!

Lastly, I would like to leave you with points to ponder over the true meaning of life and help you realize what it is like to go through winters in your life.

- Today is the oldest you have ever been, and yet the youngest you will ever be. Enjoy this day while it lasts.
- If your kids are becoming you, then your grandchildren will be perfect!
- Going out is good, but coming back home is even better!
- You forget names, but that's okay because other people forget that they even knew you! You realize you are never going to be really good at anything. Especially golf.

The things you used to care to do, you no longer care to do, but you really do care that you don't care to do them anymore.

- You sleep better on a lounge chair with the TV blaring than in bed. It's called *"pre-sleep."*
- You miss the days when everything worked with just an *"ON"* and *"OFF"* switch. You tend to use more 4 letter words on a daily basis. *"What? When? Okay."*
- Now that you can afford expensive jewelry, it's not safe to wear it anywhere.
- You notice everything they sell in stores is *"sleeveless."*
- What used to be freckles are now liver spots.
- Everybody whispers, *"You have three sizes of clothes in your closet, two of which you will never wear again."*
- But OLD is good in some things: Old Songs, Old movies, and best of all, OLD FRIENDS!! It's not what you gather, but rather what you scatter that tells what kind of life you have lived.

A Christian artist named Thomas Cole has four paintings at the Washington D.C. National Gallery of Arts that has four paintings entitled, *"The Voyage of Life."* Each one of the four panels depicts a different stage of life. Childhood, Youth, Manhood, and Old Age. The last picture for the stage of life shows an old person in a boat accompanied by a guardian angel under the dark skies pierced by brilliant sunbeams. No one knows if they will make it through these stages of life for life is uncertain. But the artist understood that for the believer, death was not something to fear but to anticipate with excitement and courage.

While we want to tarry on earth to serve God and humankind, the voyage of life inevitably takes us upward to heaven, which is far better. Death is certain for all. Denying it does no good, and it doesn't change reality. We must be ready at any moment. Jesus lived for one great purpose; that by His death and resurrection, He broke the power of the devil.

"Since the children have flesh and blood, he too shared in their humanity so that by his death he might break the power of him who holds the power of death - that is, the

*devil and free those who all their lives were held in slavery by their fear of death."-**Hebrews 2:14-15:14***

Most of the time, the fear of death holds us back from doing something in our lives. We reach a certain age where we start fearing death on a daily basis. The truth is that we should not feel enslaved by death but rather anticipate it. Death can free our souls from this earth and take us to better places if we have been good human beings. How important it is to know Him as our Savior and Lord!

How wonderful to enjoy His presence throughout the voyage of life. It is my prayer that you enjoy the life that is granted to you and remember that God will always be there for you in every step of your life. Because God is always with you, through thick and thin, and He shall be there for you even after death.

Remember to offer enough love and kindness to your closed ones as they will pass on that message to their children one day. There are a lot of people who are also afraid of living their lives to the fullest. It is important to remember that life is not something that should be feared either, but rather it should be celebrated on a daily basis.

Do your best to celebrate, and do not be afraid of letting the world know of your existence. The purpose of living this life is different for everyone, so go out there and discover your purpose. It has been there with you from the moment life was breathed into you. The only thing you have to do is discover it in all its glory.

(Afterword)
LEGACY

Every historical figure in our textbooks is known for the legacies they leave behind. It is a complete proof that a person is recognized by the way they live their lives and the values they held for mankind. Legacy is more than just what you leave behind in this world. It is a living reflection of who you are. Your legacy will always live on even if you don't. Your worth will always be determined by how you lived and the kinds of morals you implemented in your life.

Your heritage can be as small as your will to strive for achievements. The things that you leave behind can be related to each and every aspect of your personality possessed by you. You do not have to go out of your way to achieve grand things in life for them to become a part of your reflection. You can build a bigger family, a career, and a community as a part of your legacy. It is our duty to help our family and guide them to do the same.

Most of us believe that it can be harder to create legacies when we are going through so many problems in our lives. We blame ourselves, or the world, for the adversaries we go through and resort to different measures to grieve. Most people resort to alcohol, or drugs, or different things so that they can cope with the problems in their lives. However, we forget to realize that these 'coping mechanisms' only provide us with more problems in life.

Today, we see that many people around us have either become alcoholics or are on the verge of becoming alcoholics. Sometimes grief is not the only factor that contributes towards alcoholism. Social drinking is also one of the most prevailing factors that contribute to developing alcoholism. Statistically speaking, 1 out of 7 people who drink alcohol end up becoming alcoholics. About five percent of social drinkers become alcoholics.

However, the proportion differs by ethnicity. For example, few Jews become alcoholic, whereas a substantial proportion of the Irish do so. This reflects culture and beliefs rather than genetics. Orthodox Jews have a lower rate as compared to Reform Jews. As the Irish have become assimilated into U.S. society, their rate of becoming an alcoholic tends to drop.

Now, you must be wondering why I am sharing this statistic. Well, it is because alcoholism can become a legacy that can cause a great deal of grief, heartaches if a family member becomes an alcoholic. Many years ago, my uncle started social drinking, and he became an alcoholic within ten years. My maternal grandfather had a number of farms, and he lost one of the farms when he tried to help his son. My wife's father was an alcoholic, and that caused her a life filled with hardships. Her mother and siblings had to live in poverty for many years because of it. Alcoholism is a legacy no family should have to endure. You are not only causing pain to yourself but to those around you.

Word to the wise: Stay away from any alcoholic beverages!

*"Wine is a mocker, strong drink is raging: and whosoever is deceived thereby is not wise." -**King James Version (KJV) 20***

Recently our Pastor Rev. David Elkins gave a sermon entitled, *"The Calculus of the Kingdom,"* that introduced the word:

'ANAKEPHALAIOSASTHAI'

What Does It Mean to Endure?

There are many times where we are admonished in the scripture 'to endure.' But we do not really know what endurance really looks like. What does endurance look like to you? Is it smiling on the outside and still feeling unwell on the inside? Or is endurance all about bearing the pain you go through right now for a better future? Well, our answers on endurance vary due to our different perceptions. All of the answers depend on your view of the world and the nature of your sin. Your view of what it means to be a disciple of Jesus will define *"endurance"* for you. It will also define your outlook on this world as well as your future expectations.

What does ANAKEPHALAIOSASTHAI mean to you?

Now, I know that this word may not be easy to pronounce. But it does not matter how you pronounce it as long as you know what it really means.

ANAKEPHALAIOSASTHAI means, *"God made known to us the mystery of God's will, according to God's purpose, which God set forth in Christ as a plan for the fullness of time, to anakephalaiosasthai all things in him, things in heaven and things on earth."*

As long as we know that endurance depends on what we believe in relieving our pain, then our chances of choosing the wrong path in life become less.

Legacy planning is often equated to end-of-life planning, but your legacy is about so much more than merely what you intend to leave behind. It is also about how you live your life now – how you choose to spend your time, energy, and passion. Your legacy is a living reflection of what matters to you the most. It is all about your unique story, unfolding in real-time as you make progress in life.

You should always know what is present at the center of your living legacy. What do you want your legacy to be all about? While each legacy is as unique and multifaceted as the individual creating it, this dives into three areas that often matter the most: family, career, and community.

What's at the center of your living legacy?

Sometimes, the things that mean the most to us get relegated to *"someday."* We always tell ourselves that we can do it someday, but not today. However, your legacy starts from the moment you are born. It is up to you to leave an impression on people so that they can reminisce about your legacy. Imagine, instead, purposefully making room for more of what matters. Answer these questions to help bring what's important to you into focus, then discover insights on ways to live your legacy today.

For example:

- Give more generously to the causes you believe in.

- Treasure moments with loved ones, sharing stories, values, traditions, and life lessons as you move forward in life.

- Invest in your business to ensure its survival so that it can thrive even long after you are gone.

- Volunteer with organizations whose values reflect yours.

- Strike a happy balance between making a living and making a life.

- Challenge your company to give back in meaningful ways.

- Ensure that the people you cherish are taken care of in every way - now and down the road.

- Inspire friends and family to help you change the world for the better.

It is very important for you to follow these rules so that you can create your own legacy in this world. After all, legacy is more than just leaving something behind for people. It is also about leaving something in people.

Edward L. Roth, CFP ®

Ed and Millie Roth Family in 2009

Investment Planning Professional team as of 2012

Easy Ed and The Country Pals, taken on 11/1/2006

Ed Roth and Jerry Stutzman
Vocal Backup, Nancy L. Nofziger
Recorded Live at Tree Lakes Retirement Center
Bradenton, FL
1/6/2008

THE TWELVE STEPS TO A MEANINGFUL LIFE

Made in the USA
Monee, IL
15 November 2020